Tracing and Writing 0-20

2,100+ tracing units!

Arrows to show direction

Big Book of Number TRACING

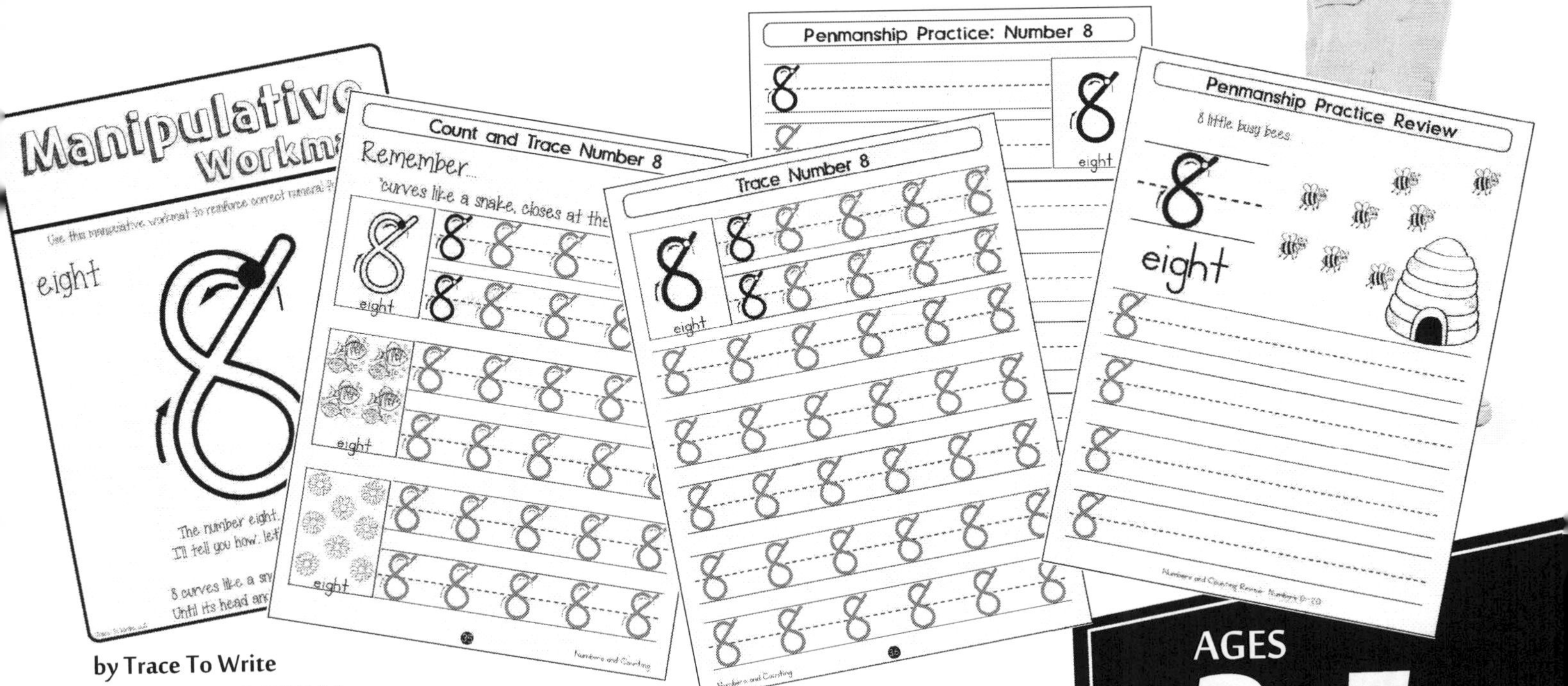

by Trace To Write

SECOND EDITION

AGES 3-5

ALIGNS WITH SCHOOL STANDARDS

SECOND EDITION
PRIMARY PENMANSHIP

GRADE K

TRACE TO WRITE, LLC, PO Box 481030, Charlotte, NC 28269.
www.trace2write.com

Printed in the United States of America.

ISBN 978-1-949210-02-6

Interior Artwork by Clever Cat Creations, Dancing Crayon Designs, Artifex

Primer Level

ALIGNS WITH SCHOOL STANDARDS

Kindergarten students are required to write numbers 0-20 and represent a number of objects with a written numeral 0-20 (with 0 representing a count of no objects). The Big Book of Number Tracing 0-20, prepares students to meet this kindergarten objective. The Big Book of Number Tracing 0-20, provides extensive focus on printed number formation for children ages 3-5. Large print is included in the text to encourage correct pencil placement while introducing formation concepts.

The full-page format presents one number per page—allowing teachers to recognize and focus on any number the student may struggle with. With over 2,100 tracing units, this workbook helps students practice writing numbers until they can form them correctly. **Guided writing lines and arrowed strokes** are included to indicate where each numeral begins and ends. Each number is presented for tracing at least 55 times before the free-hand practice page.

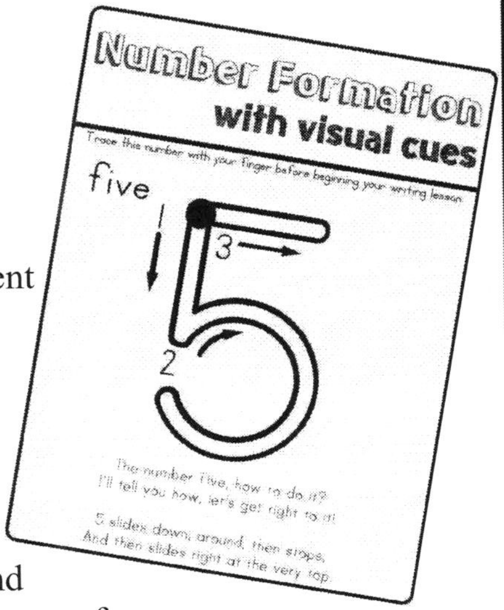

NUMBER FORMATION with Visual Cues

The Number Formation Workmats with Visual Cues, appear before each new number is introduced. The Number Formation Workmat should be used by the student as the teacher models correct numeral formation. Instruct the student to place their finger on the dot to begin, then verbally detail the direction the student should proceed in while tracing each number. The student should practice finger-tracing each number several times to become comfortable with directionality before beginning each lesson.

MANIPULATIVE WORKMATS

Manipulative Workmats are included to use with Play-Doh, beads, beans, string, Cheerios and other dry materials. The workmats provide a fun way for students to learn numeral formation while also helping to strengthen motor skills.

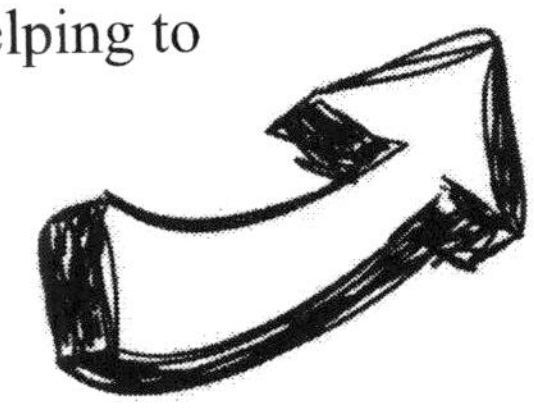

NUMBER FORMATION POEMS

Number formation poems are included before each 0-10 tracing lesson to help students understand the way numerals 0-10 are formed. Similarly, the formation poems for numerals 11-20 help students learn which single digit numbers are paired together to form numerals 11-20.

Includes arrows to show direction

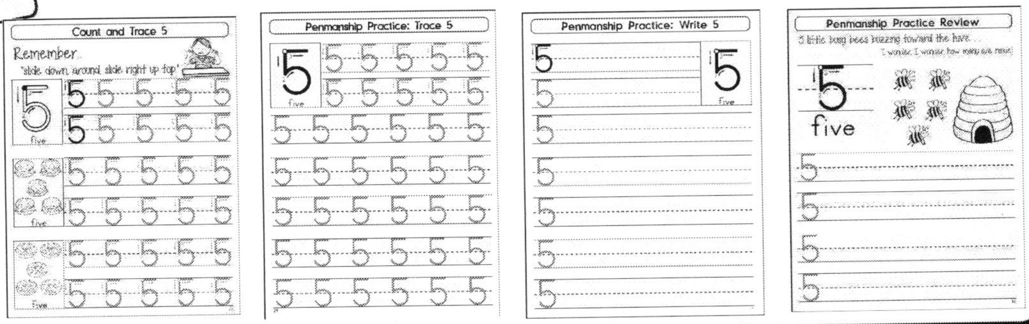

Number Formation
with visual cues

Trace this number with your finger before beginning your writing lesson.

zero

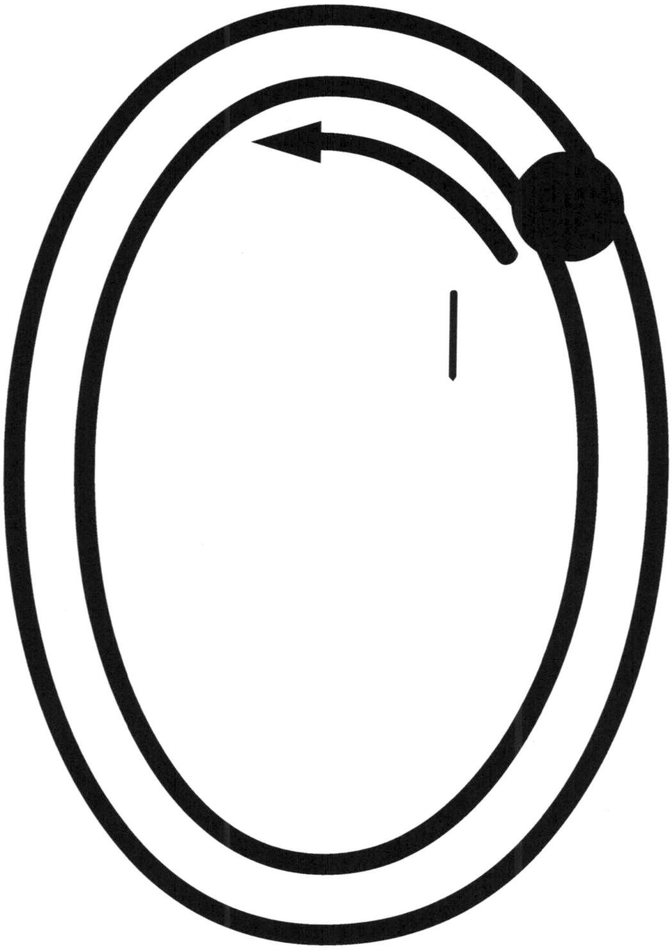

The number zero, how to do it?
I'll tell you how, let's get right to it!

This number is our invisible hero,
Fly around in a loop to make a zero.

Count and Trace 0

Remember...

"loop around to make a zero."

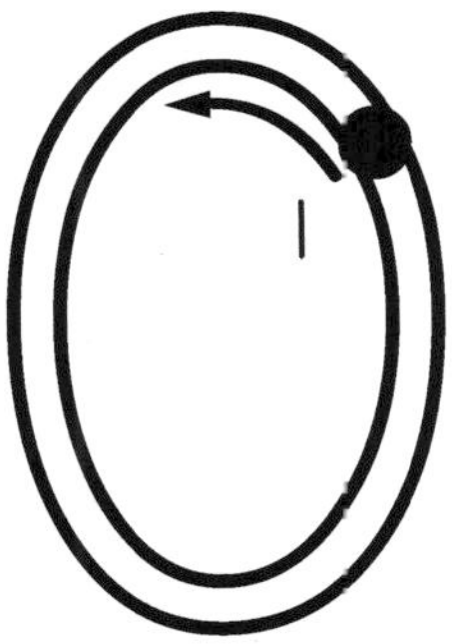

zero

zero

zero

Penmanship Practice: Trace 0

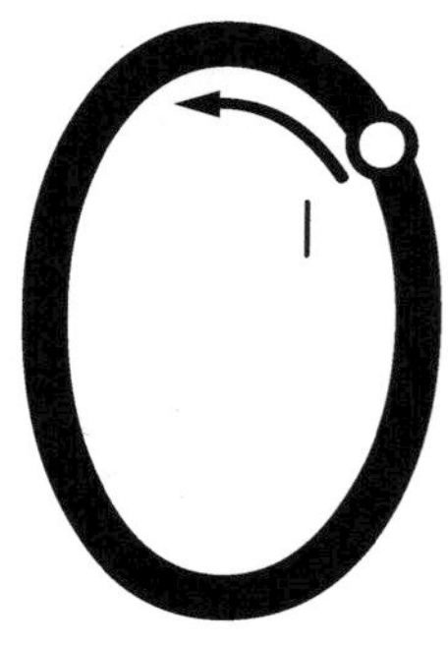

zero

Penmanship Practice: Write 0

zero

Number Formation
with visual cues

Trace this number with your finger before beginning your writing lesson.

one

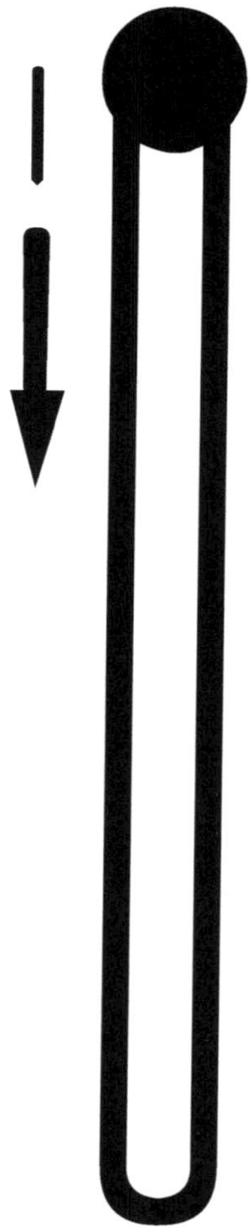

The number one, how to do it?
I'll tell you how, let's get right to it!

One straight line, sky to ground,
Not bottom up, but top down.

Count and Trace 1

Remember...

"one line down, sky to ground."

one

one

one

Penmanship Practice: Trace 1

one

Penmanship Practice: Write 1

one

Number Formation

with visual cues

Trace this number with your finger before beginning your writing lesson.

two

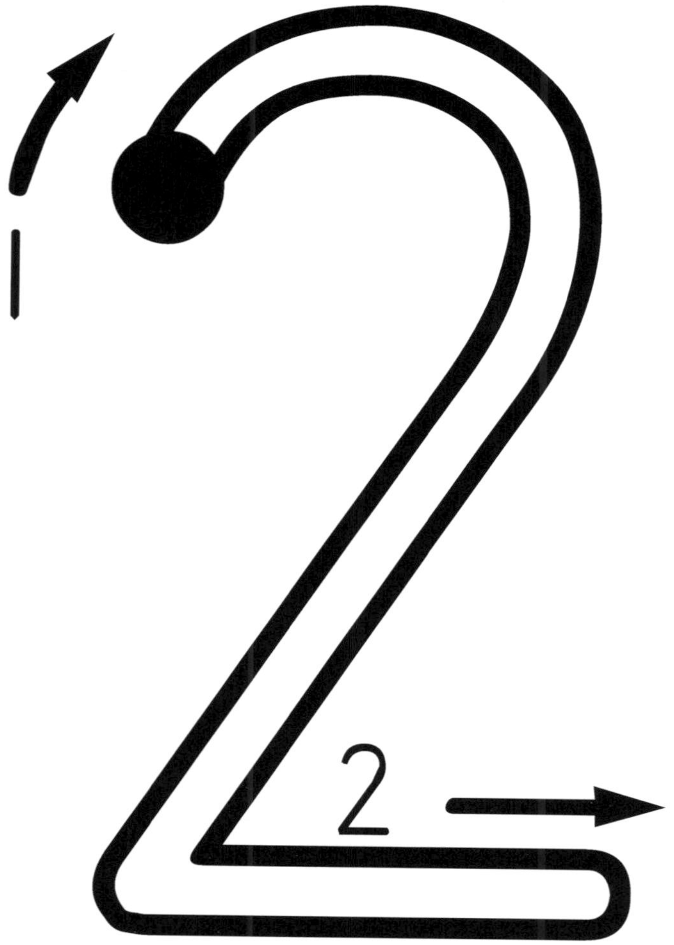

The number two, how to do it?
I'll tell you how, let's get right to it!

Two buzzes up and around like a bee in flight,
Once at the bottom, it buzzes straight right.

Count and Trace 2

Remember...

"buzz up and around, then out."

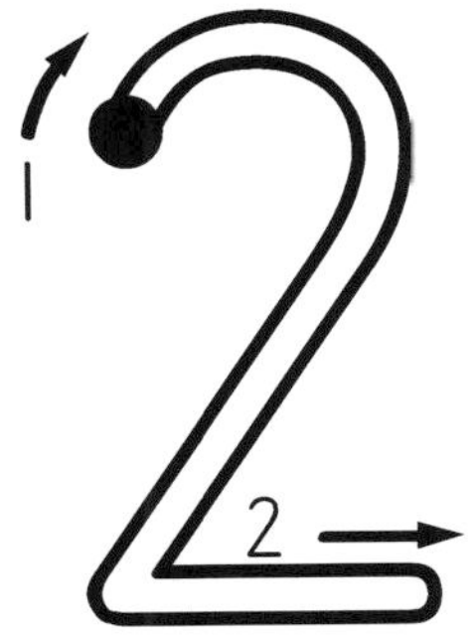

two

2 2 2 2 2

2 2 2 2 2

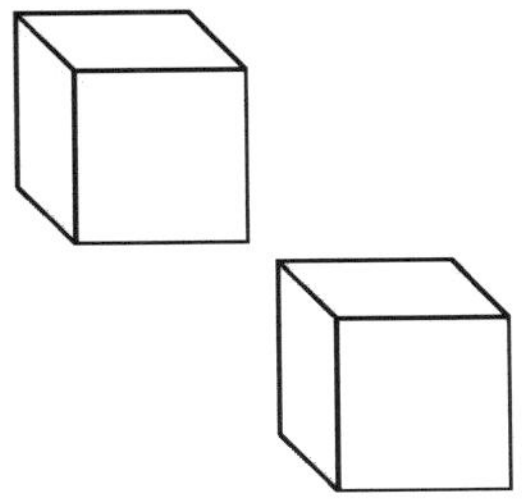

two

2 2 2 2 2

2 2 2 2 2

two

2 2 2 2 2

2 2 2 2 2

Penmanship Practice: Trace 2

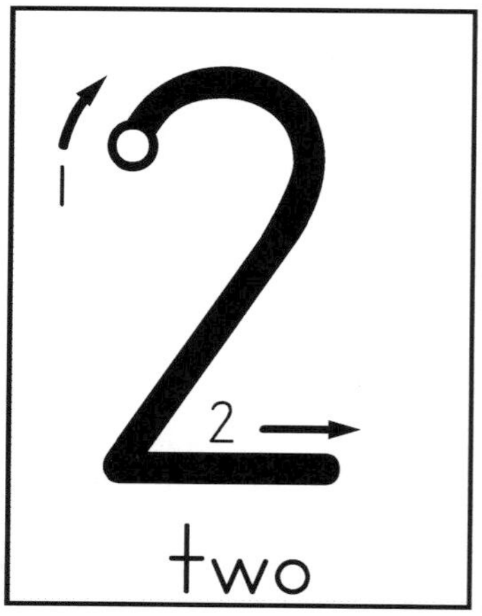

Penmanship Practice: Write 2

2

two

2

2

2

2

2

2

2

Number Formation
with visual cues

Trace this number with your finger before beginning your writing lesson.

three

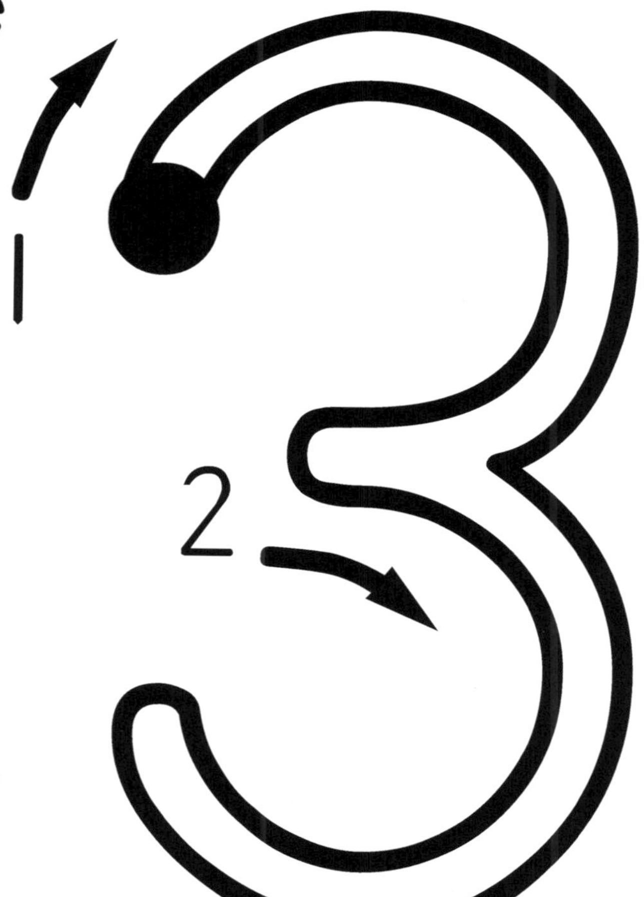

The number three, how to do it?
I'll tell you how, let's get right to it!

3's top matches its bottom,
Curve around twice and you've got it!

Count and Trace 3

Remember...

"3's top matches its bottom."

three

3 3 3 3 3

3 3 3 3 3

three

3 3 3 3 3

3 3 3 3 3

three

3 3 3 3 3

3 3 3 3 3

Penmanship Practice: Trace 3

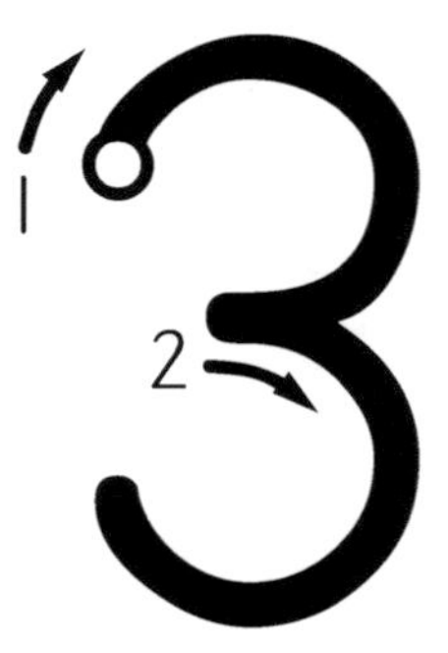

three

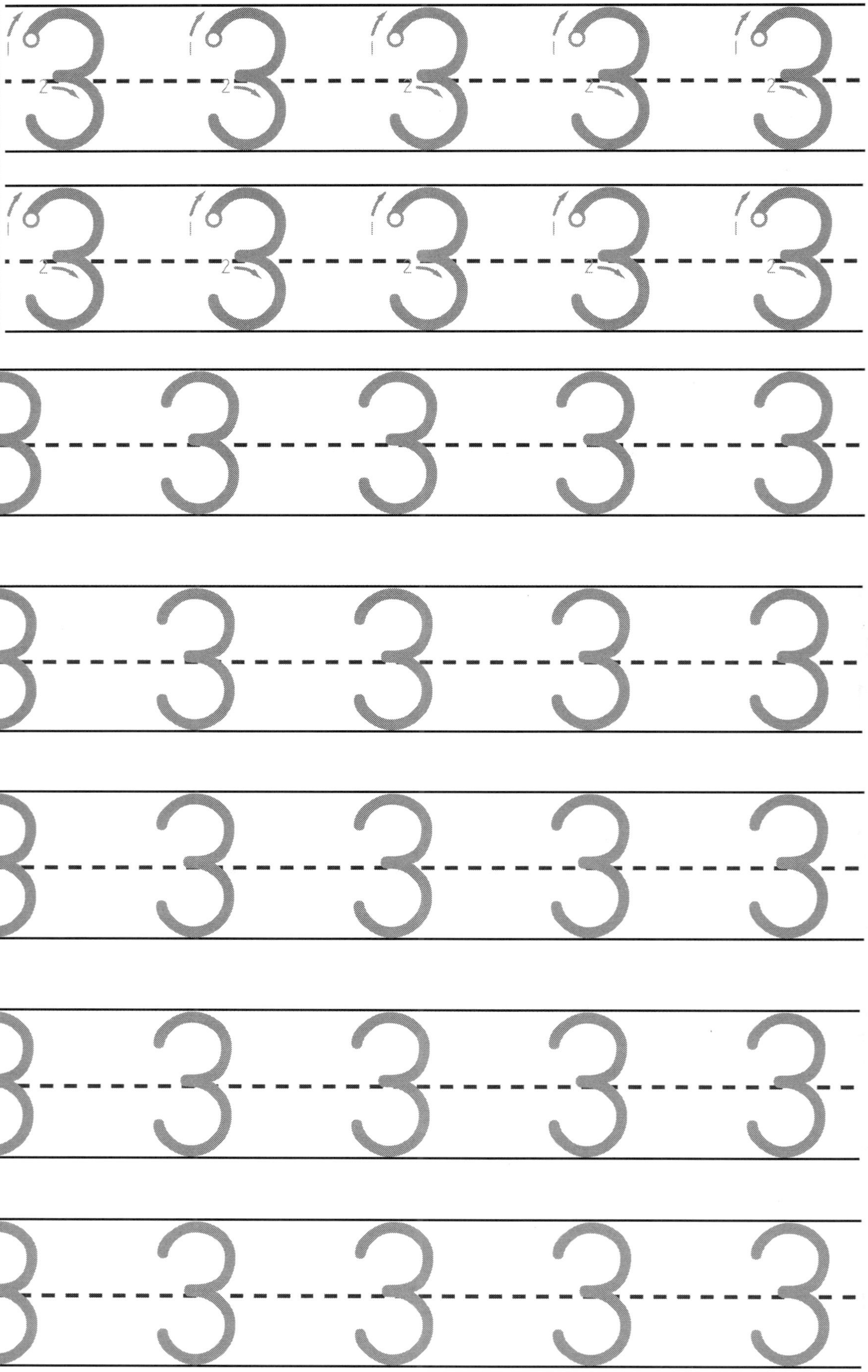

Penmanship Practice: Write 3

1 2 3

3

3

3

3

3

3

1 2 3

three

Number Formation

with visual cues

Trace this number with your finger before beginning your writing lesson.

four

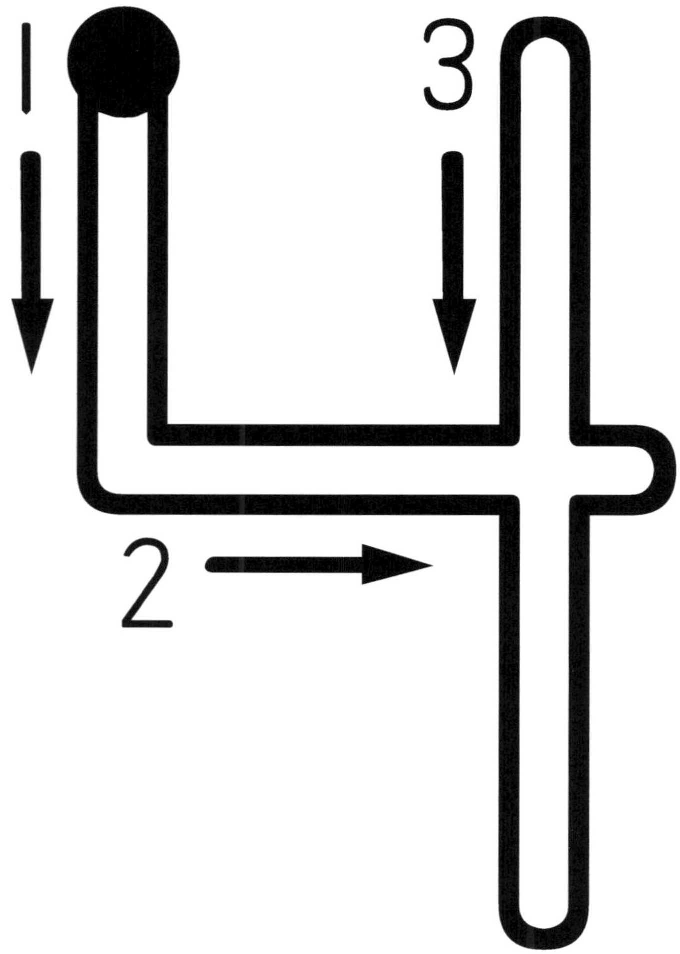

The number four, how to do it?
I'll tell you how, let's get right to it!

4's front lines form a capital "L",
Its back line is like a long straight nail.

Count and Trace 4

Remember...

"it's a capital L and long straight nail."

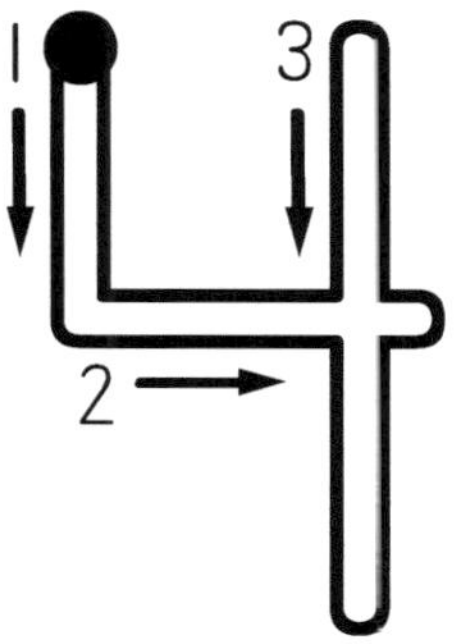

four

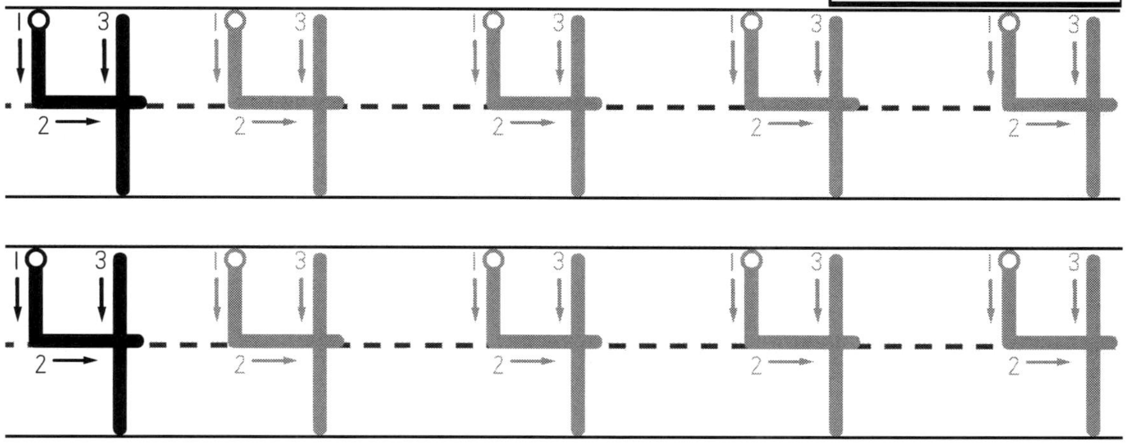

four

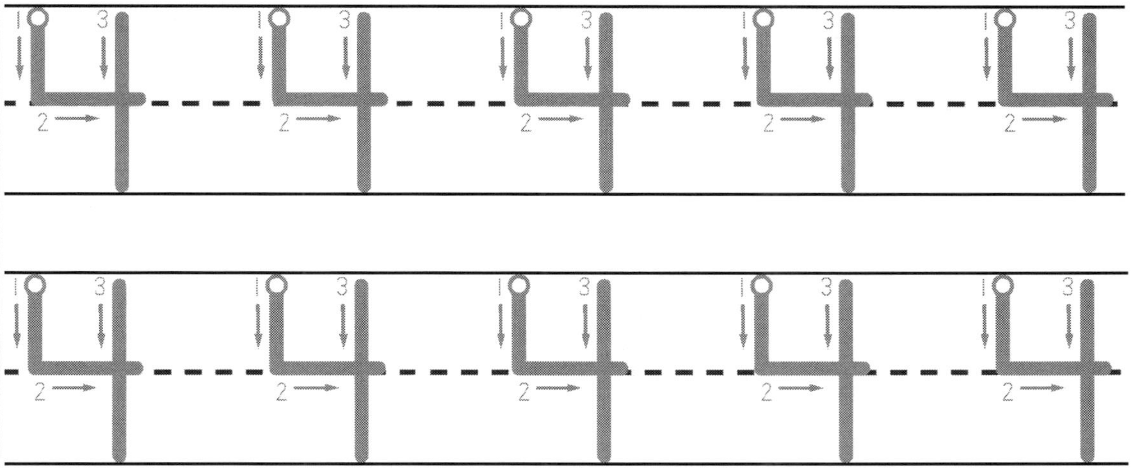

four

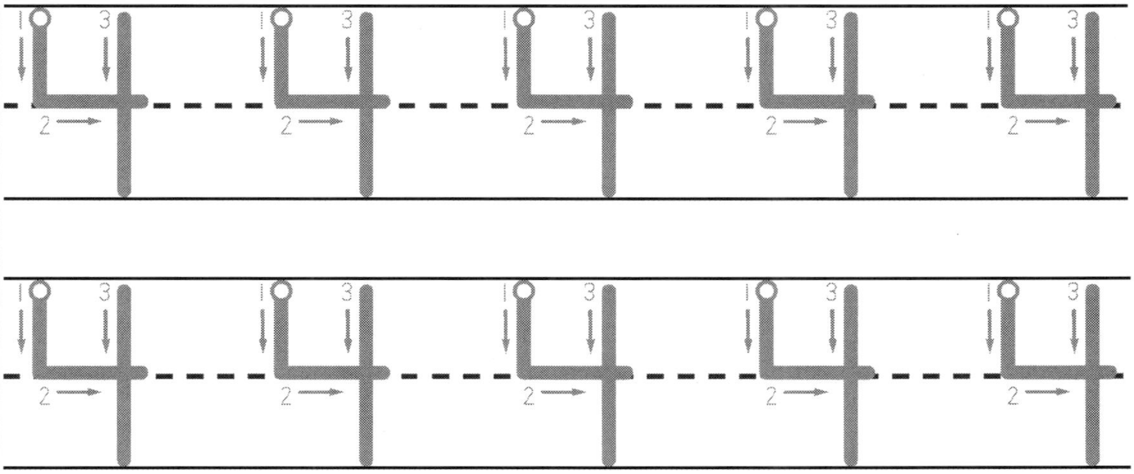

Penmanship Practice: Trace 4

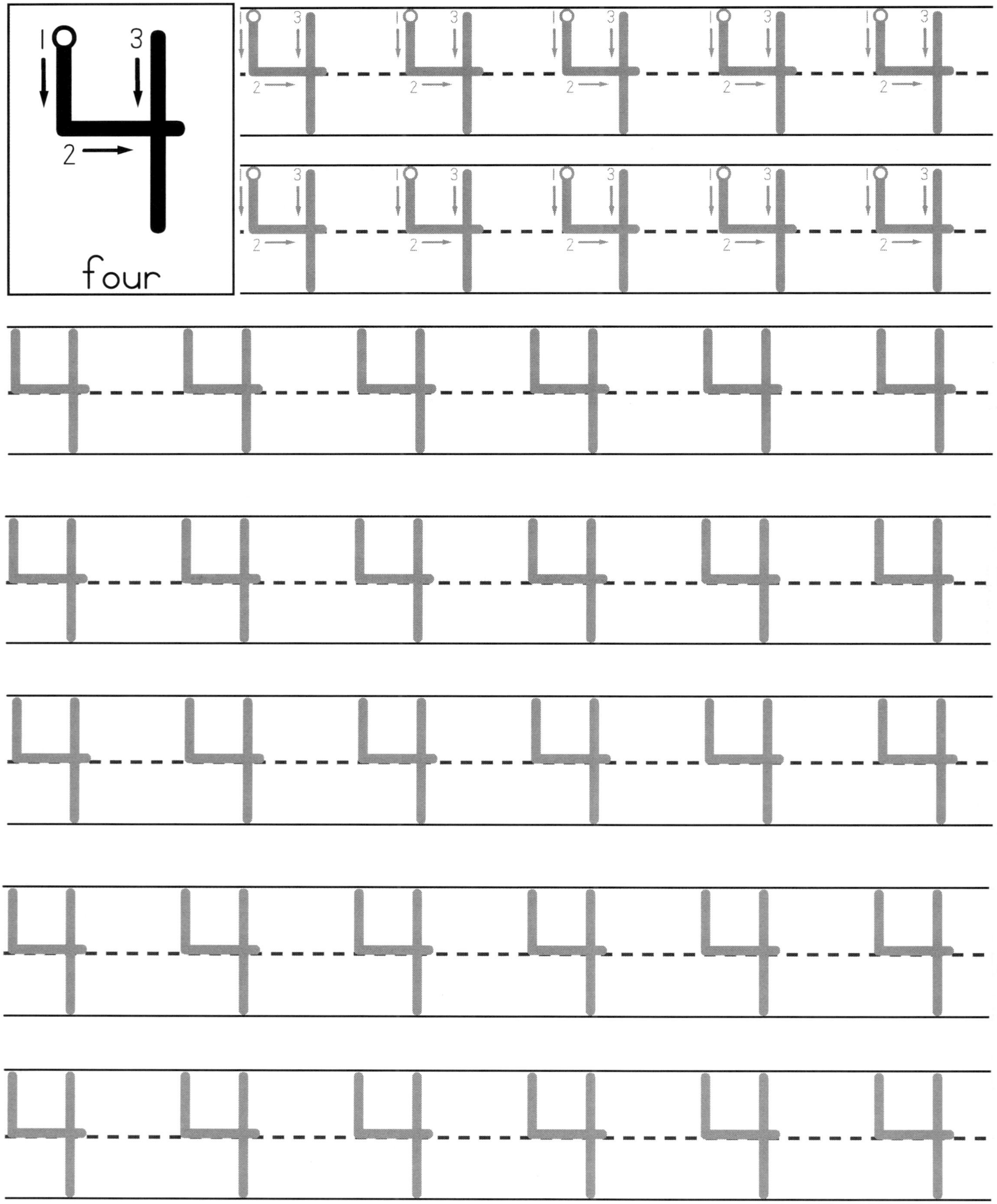

Penmanship Practice: Write 4

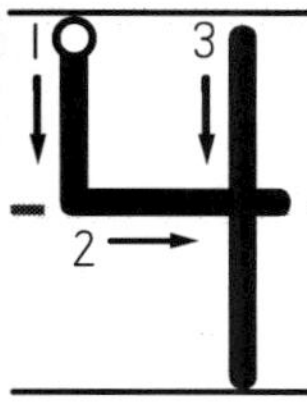

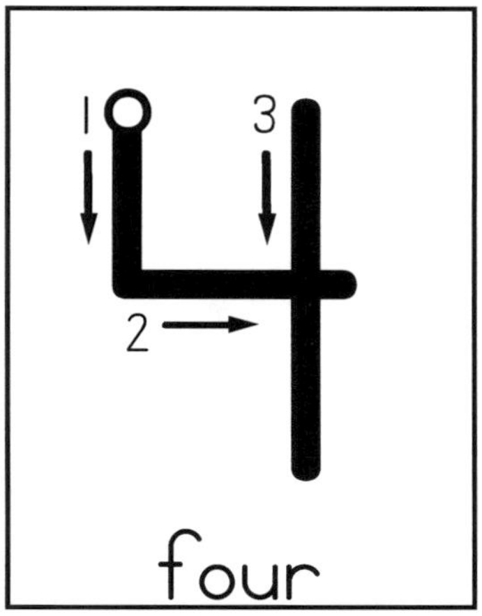

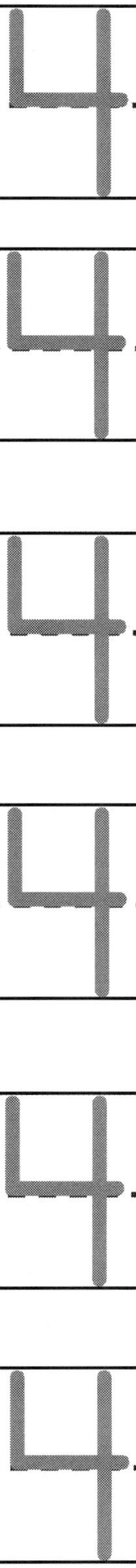

Number Formation
with visual cues

Trace this number with your finger before beginning your writing lesson.

five

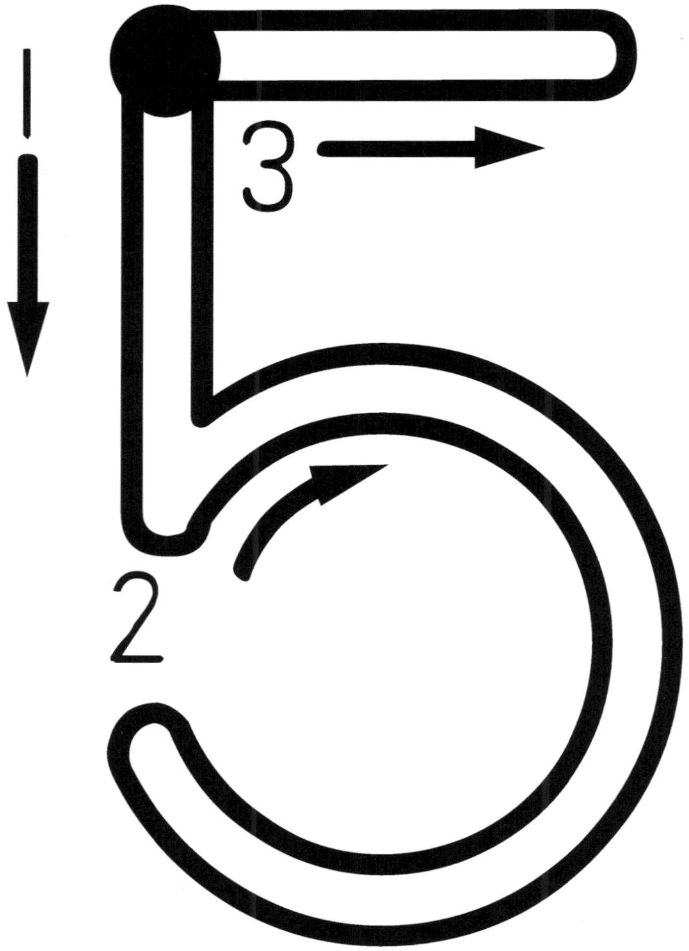

The number five, how to do it?
I'll tell you how, let's get right to it!

5 slides down, around, then stops,
And then slides right at the very top.

Count and Trace 5

Remember...

"slide down, around, slide right up top."

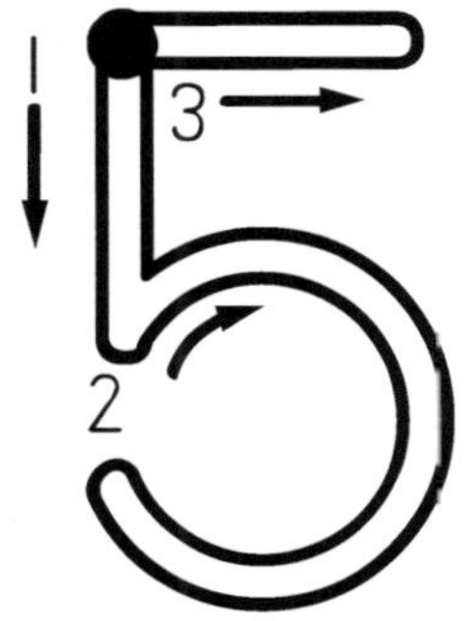

five

five

five

Penmanship Practice: Trace 5

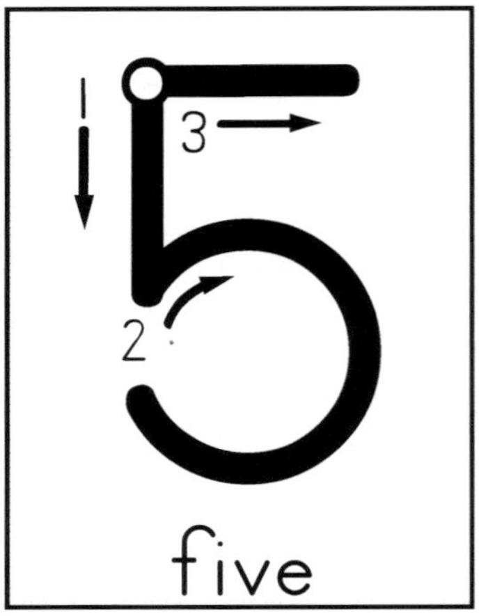

5 5 5 5 5

5 5 5 5 5

5 5 5 5 5 5

5 5 5 5 5 5

5 5 5 5 5 5

5 5 5 5 5 5

5 5 5 5 5 5

Penmanship Practice: Write 5

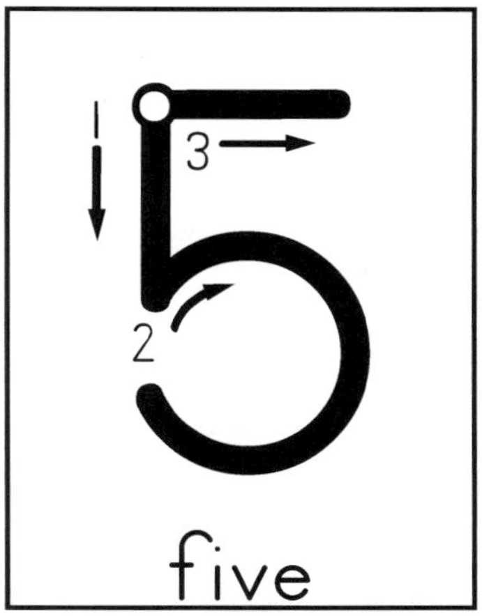

Number Formation
with visual cues

Trace this number with your finger before beginning your writing lesson.

six

The number six, how to do it?
I'll tell you how, let's get right to it!

6 swoops down and back up until it closes,
Please shut its door, don't leave it open.

Count and Trace 6

Remember...

"loop around, up, then close."

six

6 6 6 6 6

6 6 6 6 6

six

6 6 6 6 6

6 6 6 6 6

six

6 6 6 6 6

6 6 6 6 6

Penmanship Practice: Trace 6

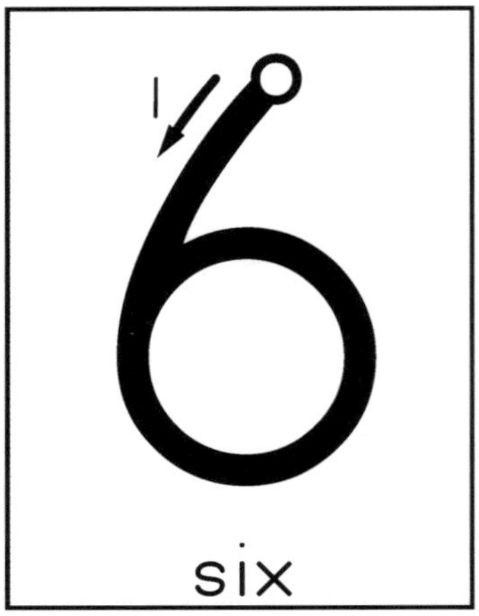

6 6 6 6 6

6 6 6 6 6

6 6 6 6 6 6

6 6 6 6 6 6

6 6 6 6 6 6

6 6 6 6 6 6

6 6 6 6 6 6

Penmanship Practice: Write 6

6

six

6

6

6

6

6

6

6

Number Formation
with visual cues

Trace this number with your finger before beginning your writing lesson.

seven

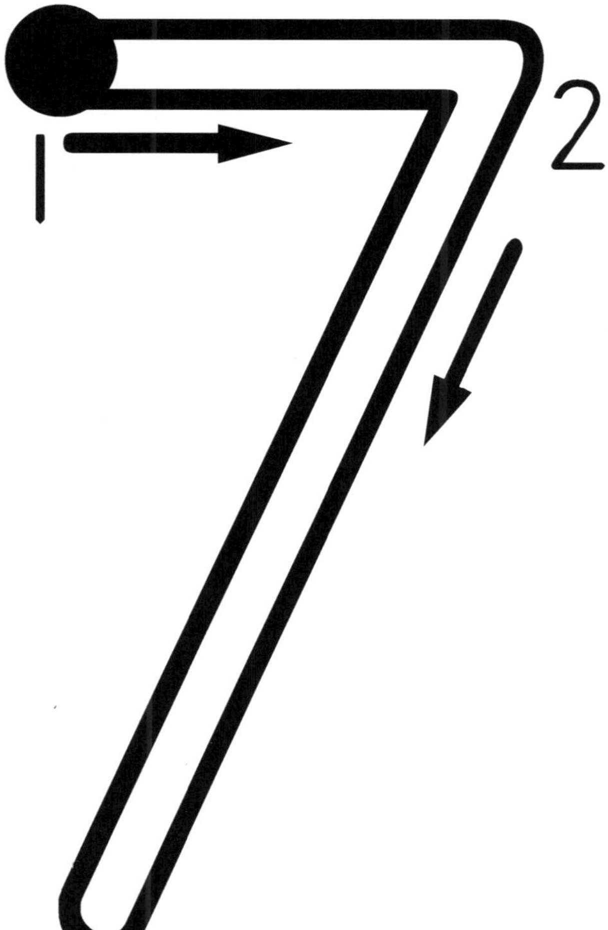

The number seven, how to do it?
I'll tell you how, let's get right to it!

7's top line slides straight across,
Then slants down to finish off.

Count and Trace 7

Remember...

"slide right, then slant down."

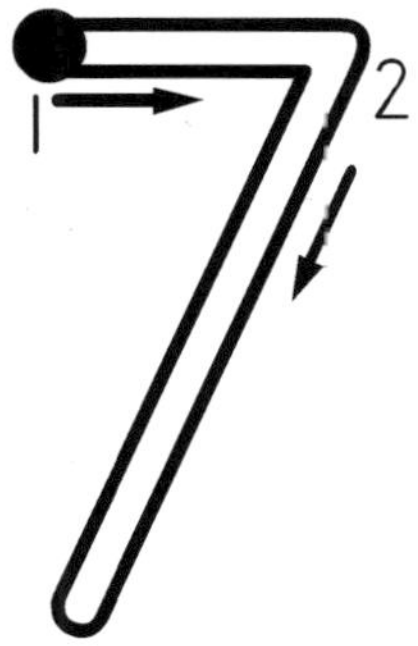

seven

seven

seven

Penmanship Practice: Trace 7

Penmanship Practice: Write 7

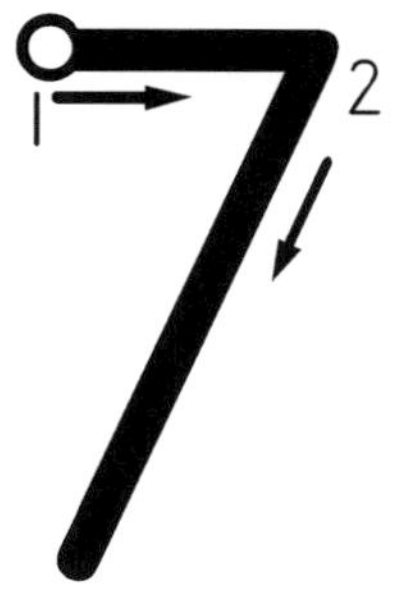

seven

Number Formation
with visual cues

Trace this number with your finger before beginning your writing lesson.

eight

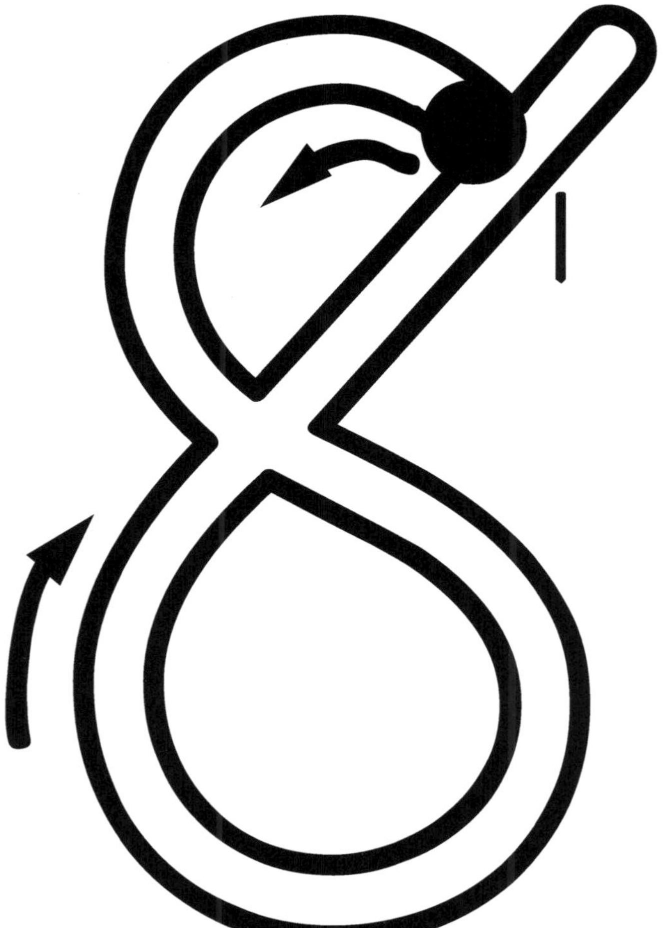

The number eight, how to do it?
I'll tell you how, let's get right to it!

8 curves like a snake and doesn't stop,
Until its head and tail meet at the top.

Count and Trace 8

Remember...

"curves like a snake, closes at the top."

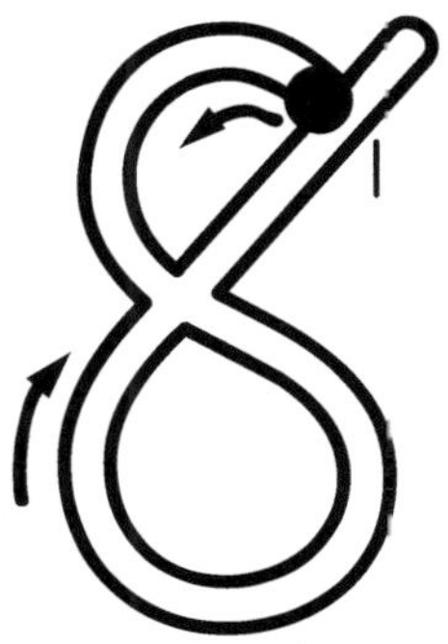

eight

eight

eight

Penmanship Practice: Trace 8

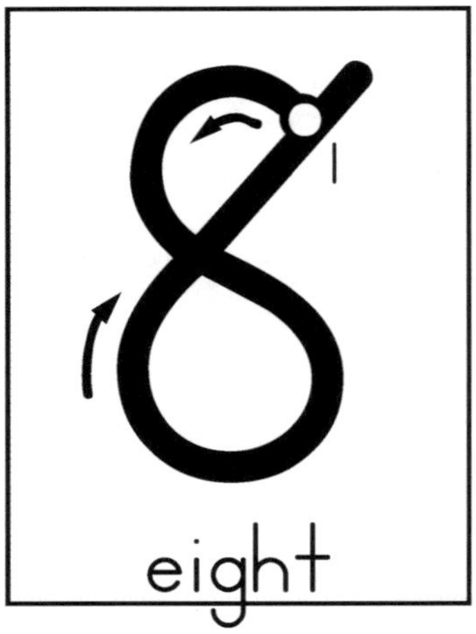

Penmanship Practice: Write 8

Number Formation
with visual cues

Trace this number with your finger before beginning your writing lesson.

nine

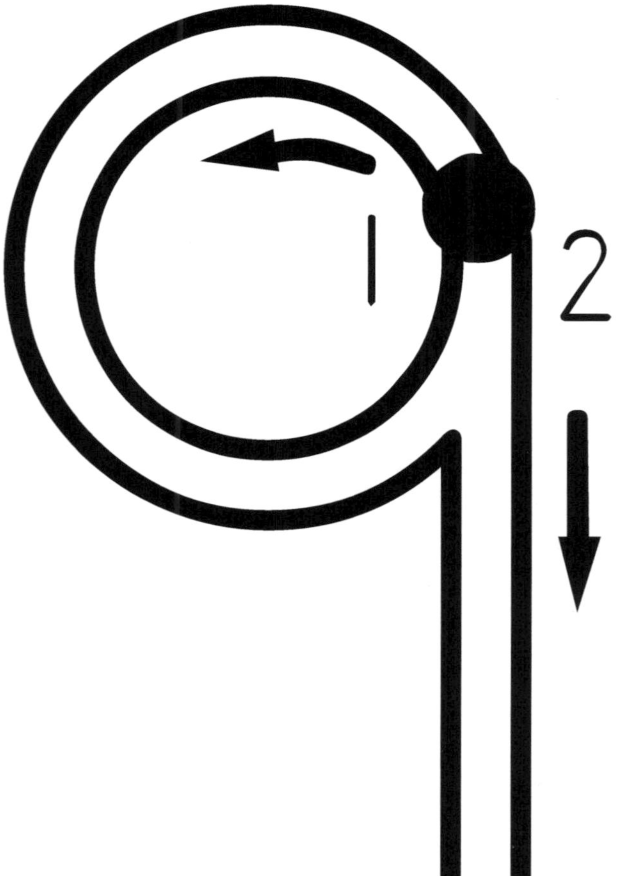

The number nine, how to do it?
I'll tell you how, let's get right to it!

9 has a circle head,
With a body that's just one straight leg.

Count and Trace 9

Remember...

"circle head and straight leg body."

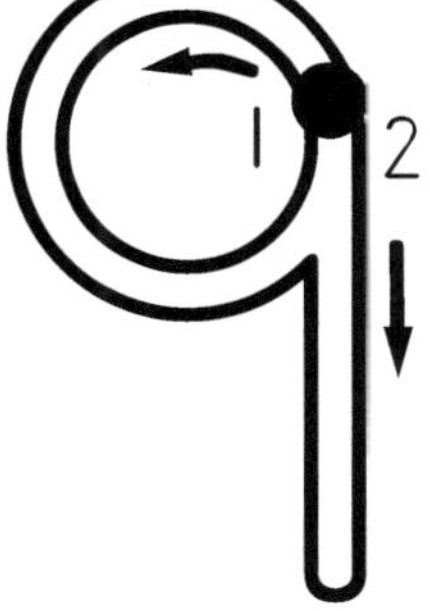

nine

nine

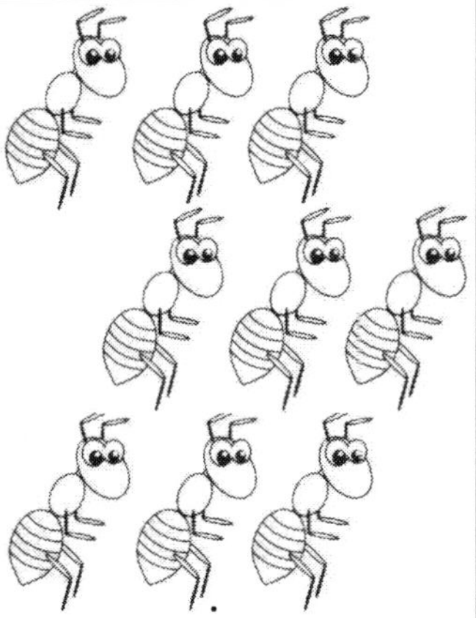

nine

Penmanship Practice: Trace 9

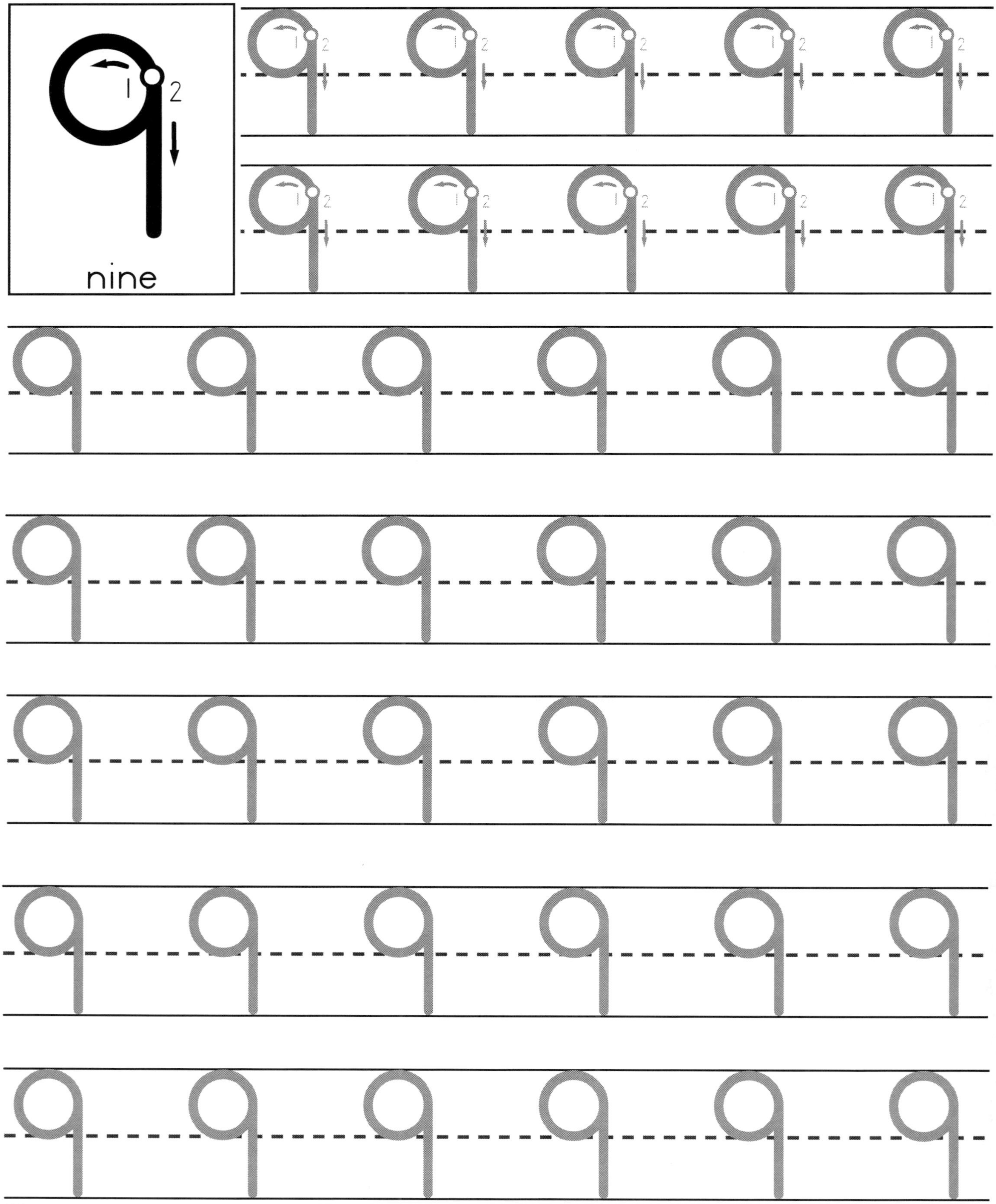

Penmanship Practice: Write 9

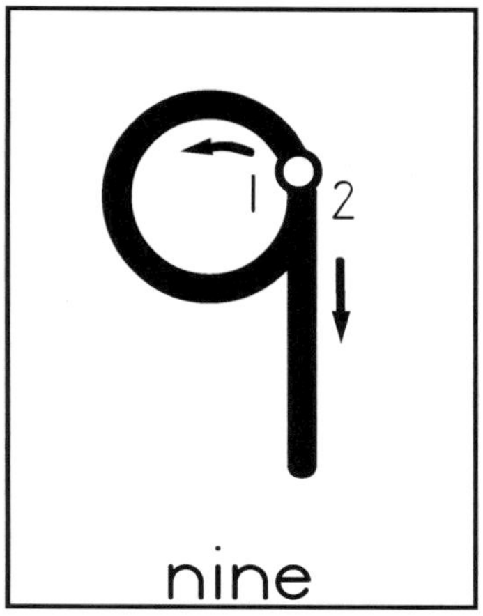

Number Formation
with visual cues

Trace this number with your finger before beginning your writing lesson.

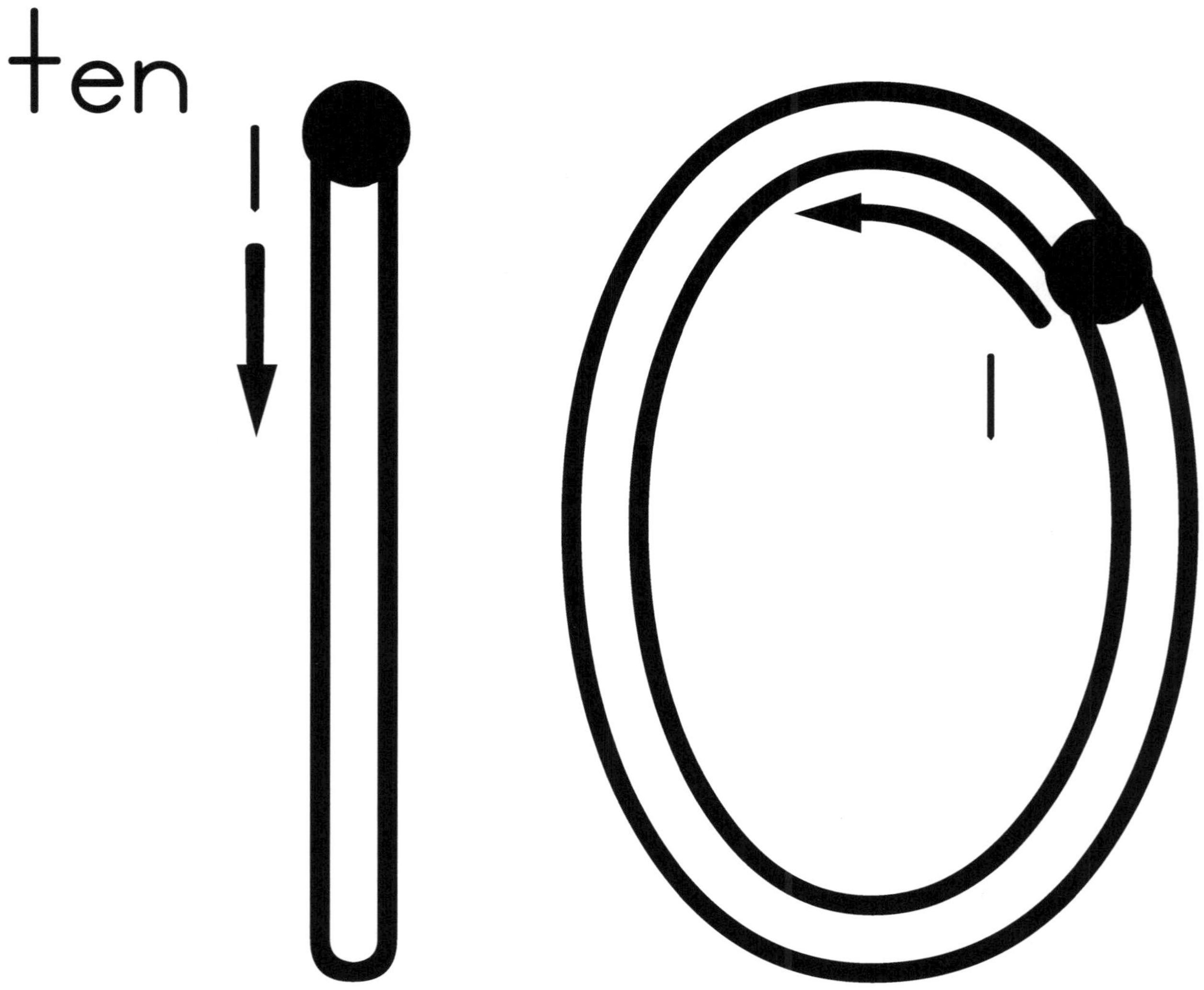

The number ten, how to do it?
I'll tell you how, let's get right to it!

10 brings back familiar friends,
1 and 0 here again!

Count and Trace 10

Remember...

"familiar friends 1 and 0."

10

ten

10 10 10 10

10 10 10 10

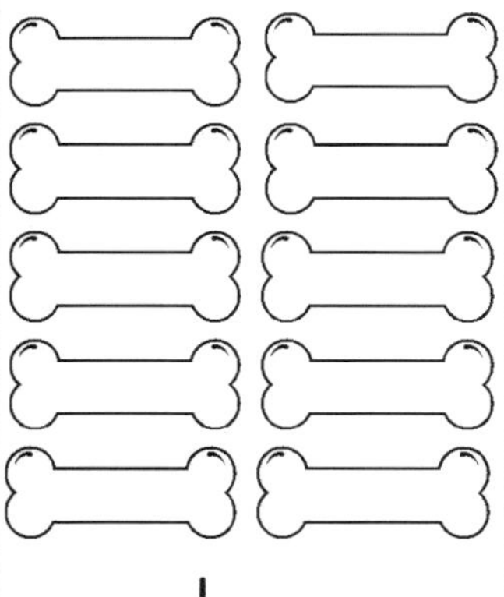

ten

10 10 10 10

10 10 10 10

ten

10 10 10 10

10 10 10 10

Penmanship Practice: Trace 10

10

ten

10 10 10

10 10 10

10 10 10 10

10 10 10 10

10 10 10 10

10 10 10 10

10 10 10 10

Penmanship Practice: Write 10

10

10

10 ten

10

10

10

10

10

Number Formation
with visual cues

Trace this number with your finger before beginning your writing lesson.

eleven

"Numbers 11-20, just like ten,
Are made up of number friends!"

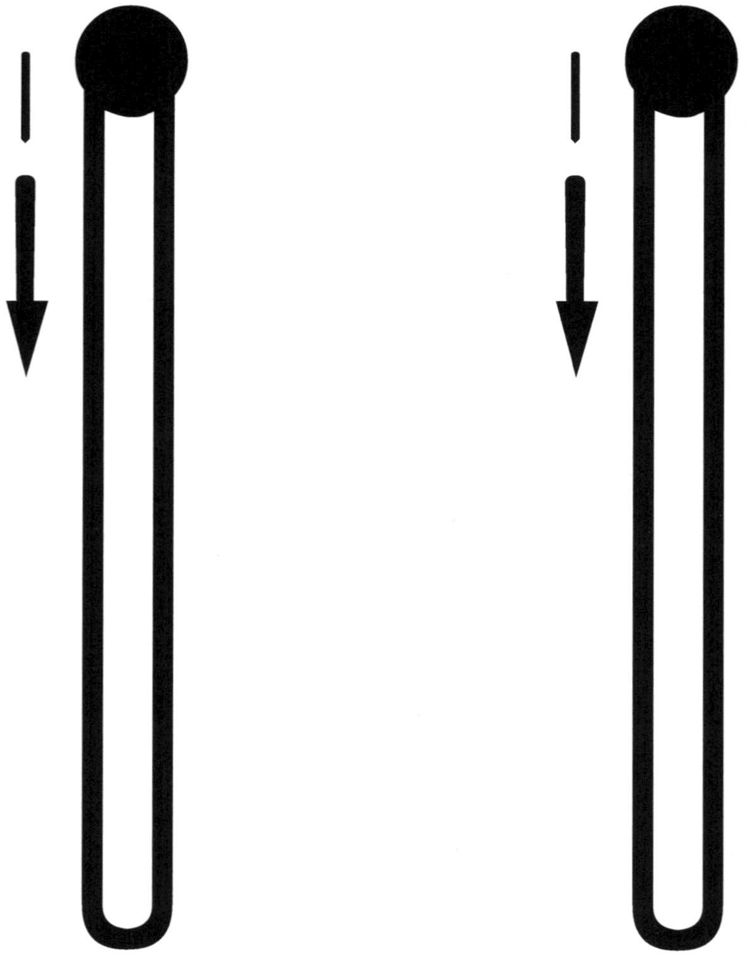

Two straight lines and then you're done,
Eleven is just a 1 and 1.

Count and Trace 11

Ants on a hill...

Eleven little ants preparing winter's store,
One ant shouts, "We need one more!"

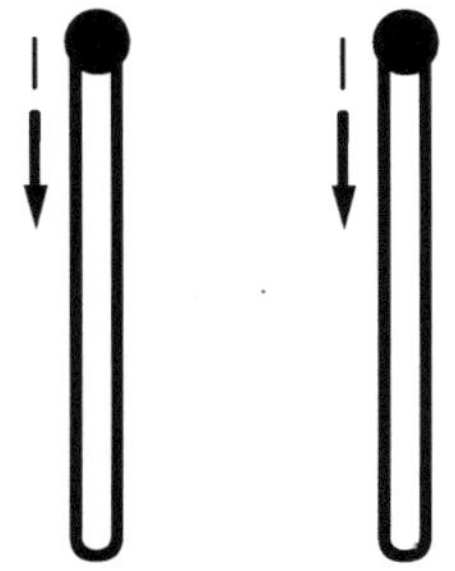

eleven

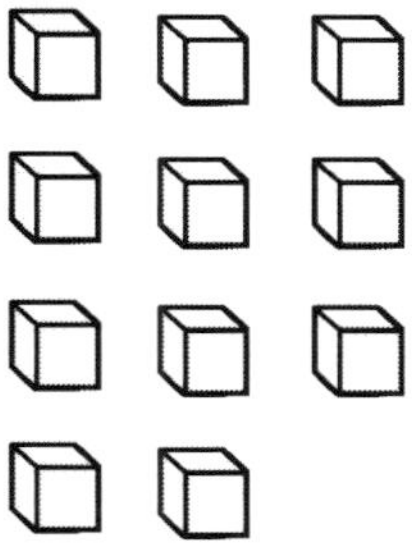

eleven

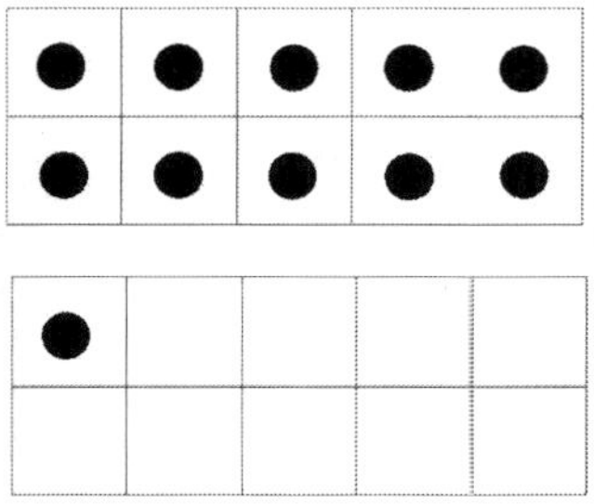

eleven

Penmanship Practice: Trace 11

eleven

Penmanship Practice: Write 11

11

eleven

Number Formation
with visual cues

Trace this number with your finger before beginning your writing lesson.

twelve

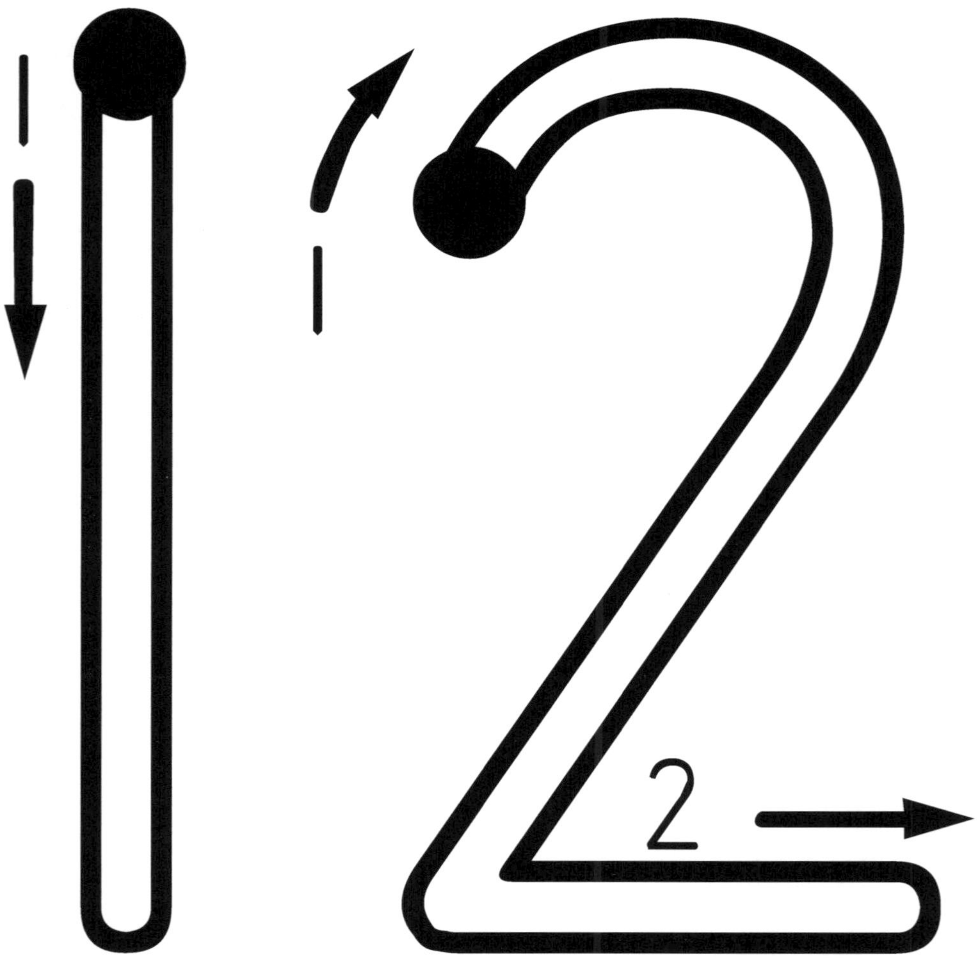

Making twelve isn't hard to do,
Just write numbers 1 and 2.

Count and Trace 12

Ants on a hill...

Twelve little ants preparing winter's store,
One ant shouts, "We need one more!"

12

twelve

12 12 12 12

12 12 12 12

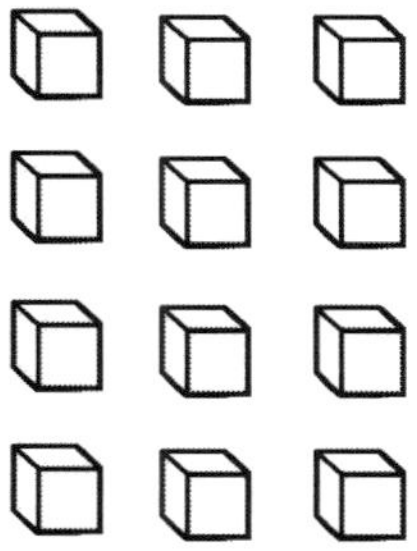

twelve

12 12 12 12

12 12 12 12

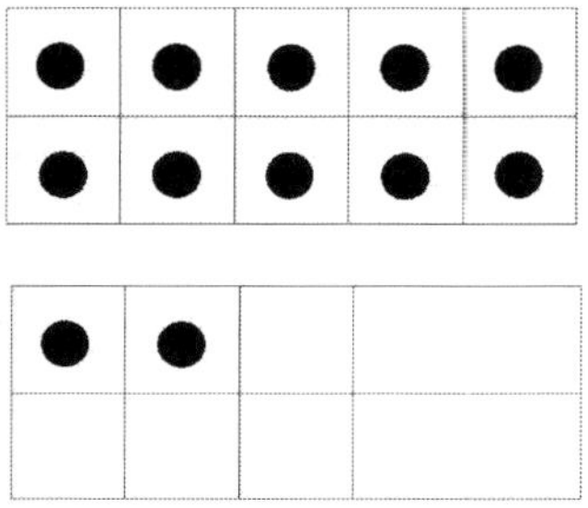

twelve

12 12 12 12

12 12 12 12

Penmanship Practice: Trace 12

12

twelve

Penmanship Practice: Write 12

12

12

12

12

12

12

12

12

twelve

Number Formation
with visual cues

Trace this number with your finger before beginning your writing lesson.

thirteen

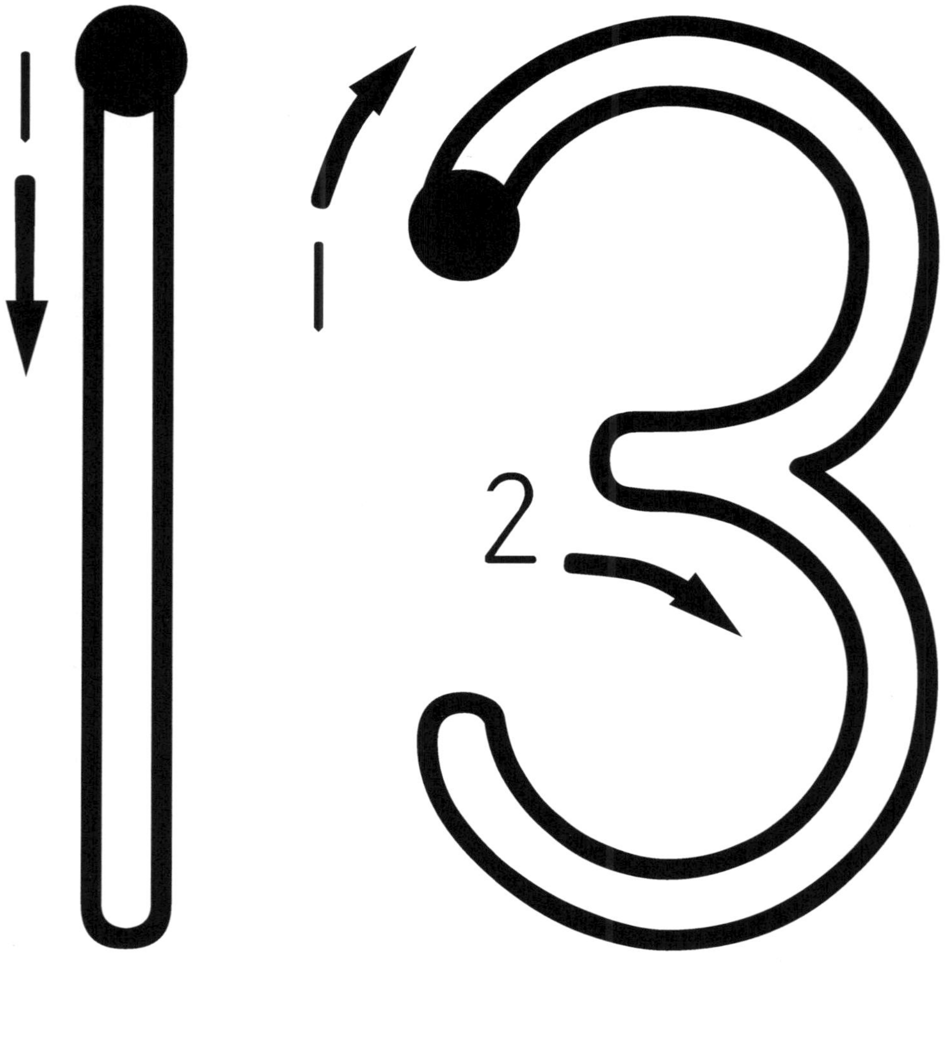

Thirteen squished close is a capital "B",
But pulled apart, it's 1 and 3.

Count and Trace 13

Ants on a hill...

Thirteen little ants preparing winter's store,
One ant shouts, "We need one more!"

13

thirteen

13 13 13 13

13 13 13 13

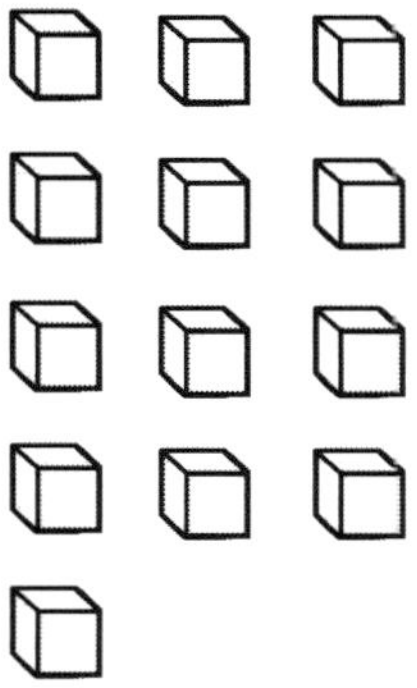

thirteen

13 13 13 13

13 13 13 13

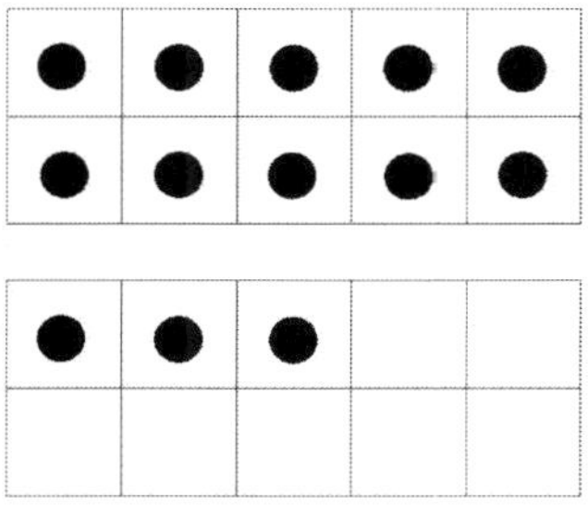

thirteen

13 13 13 13

13 13 13 13

Penmanship Practice: Trace 13

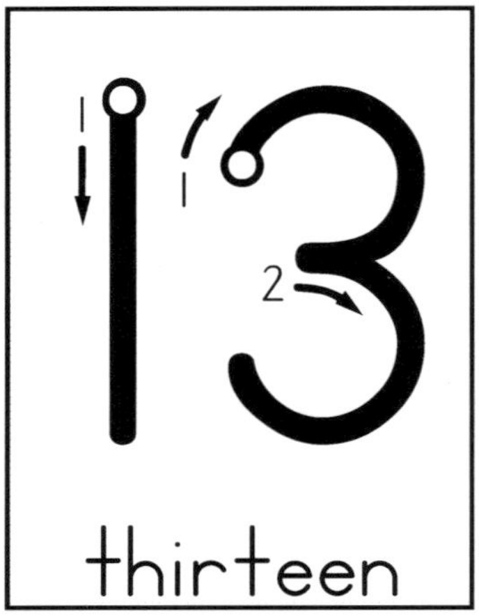

13 13 13 13

13 13 13 13

13 13 13 13 13

13 13 13 13 13

13 13 13 13 13

13 13 13 13 13

13 13 13 13 13

Penmanship Practice: Write 13

13

13

13

13

13

13

13

13

thirteen

Number Formation
with visual cues

Trace this number with your finger before beginning your writing lesson.

fourteen

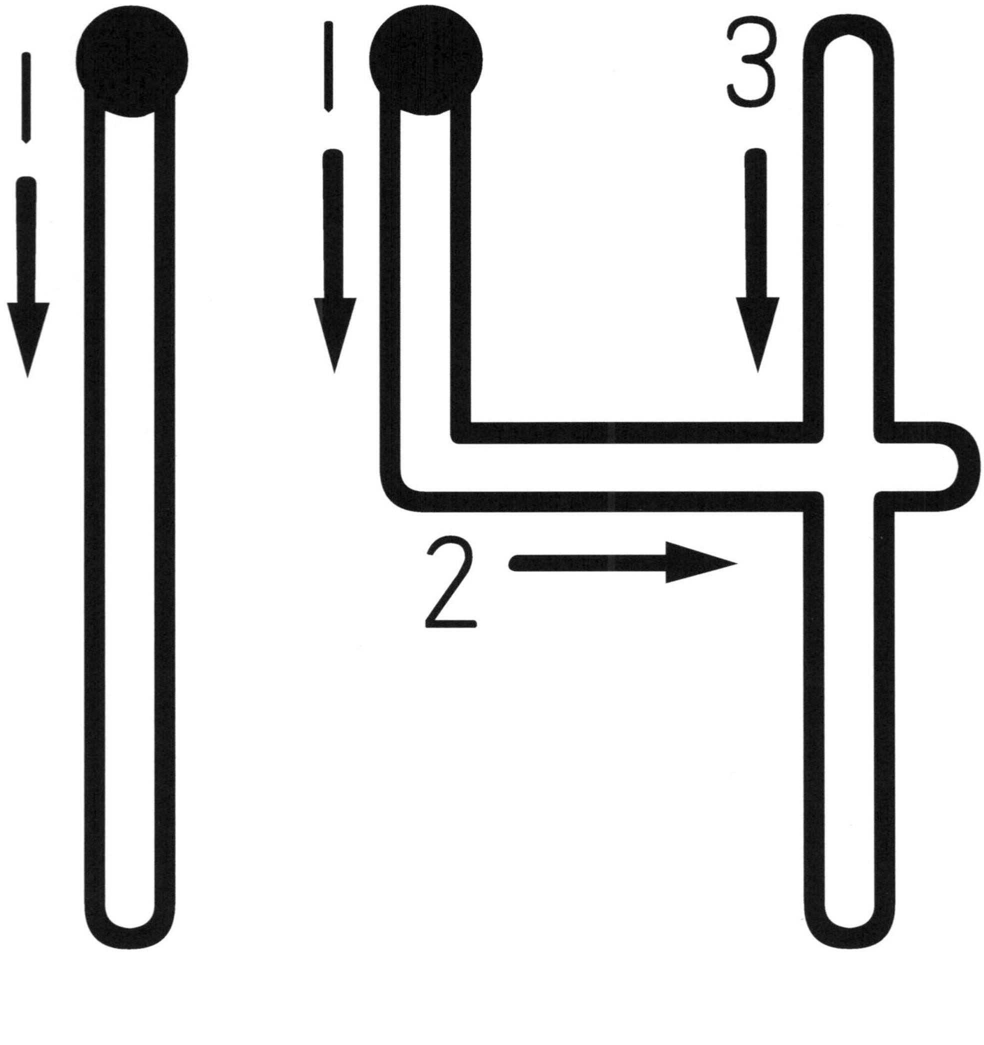

Fourteen doesn't take much more,
Than joining numbers 1 and 4.

Count and Trace 14

Ants on a hill...

Fourteen little ants preparing winter's store,
One ant shouts, "We need one more!"

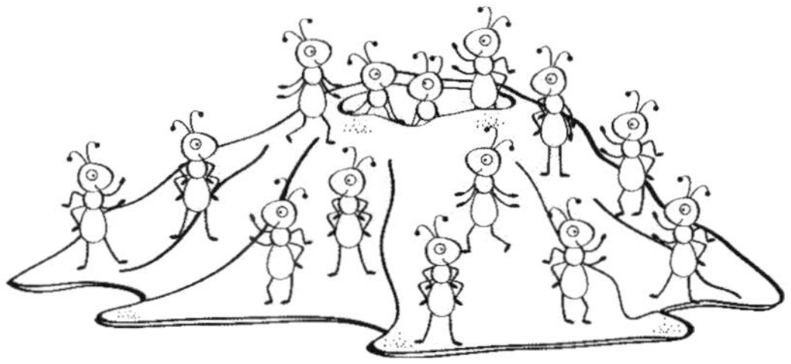

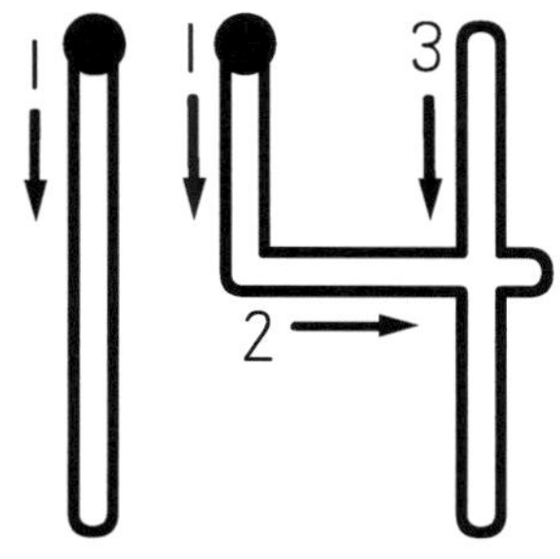

fourteen

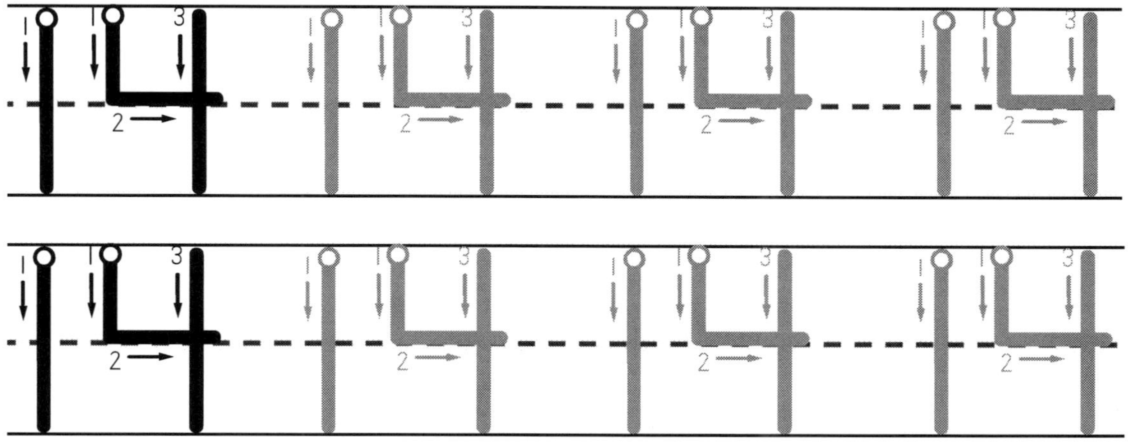

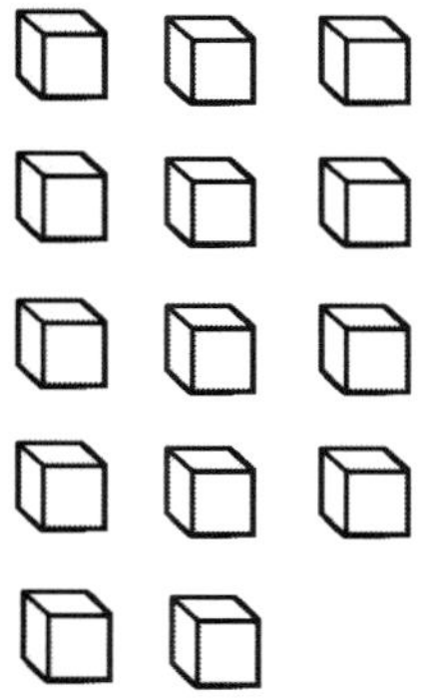

fourteen

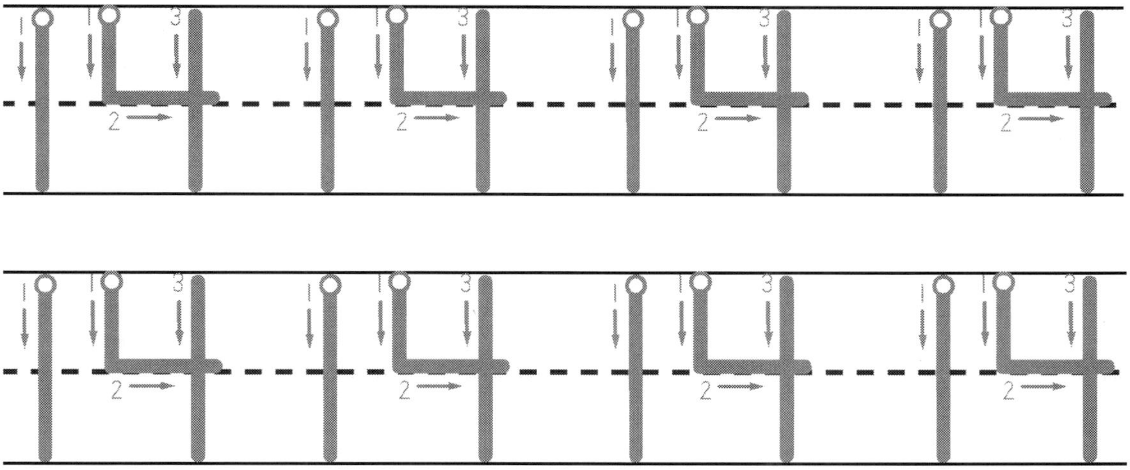

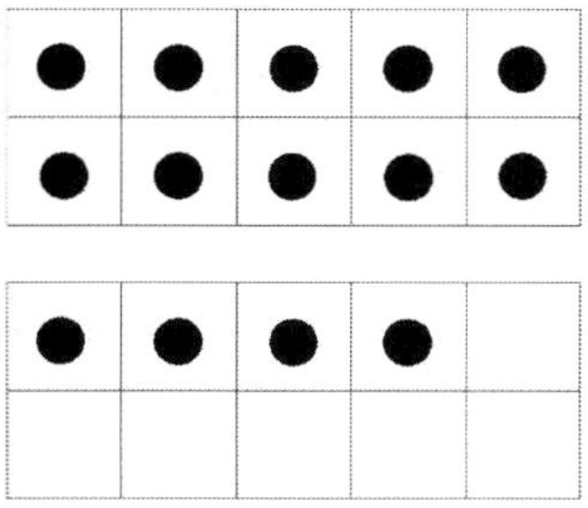

fourteen

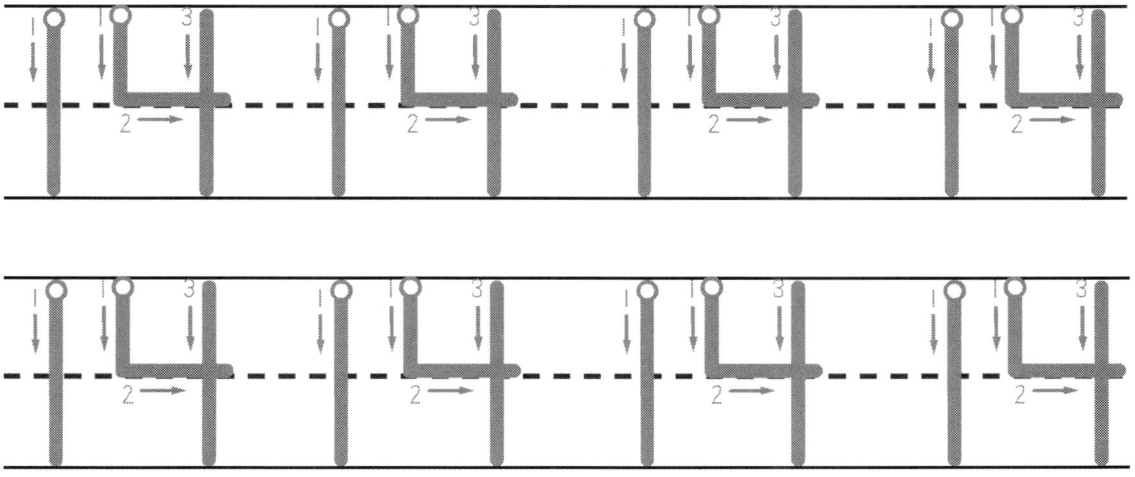

Penmanship Practice: Trace 14

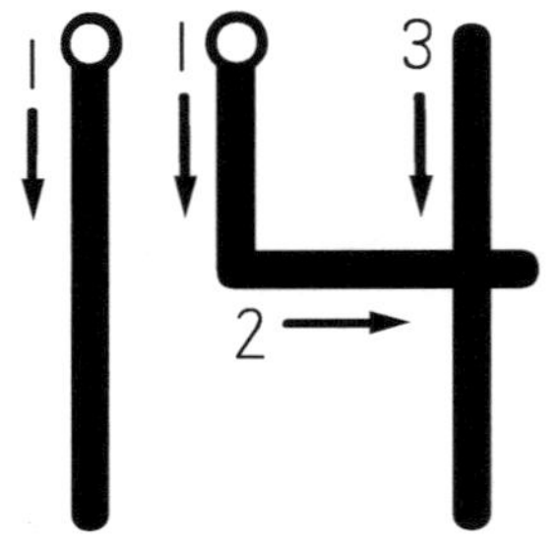

fourteen

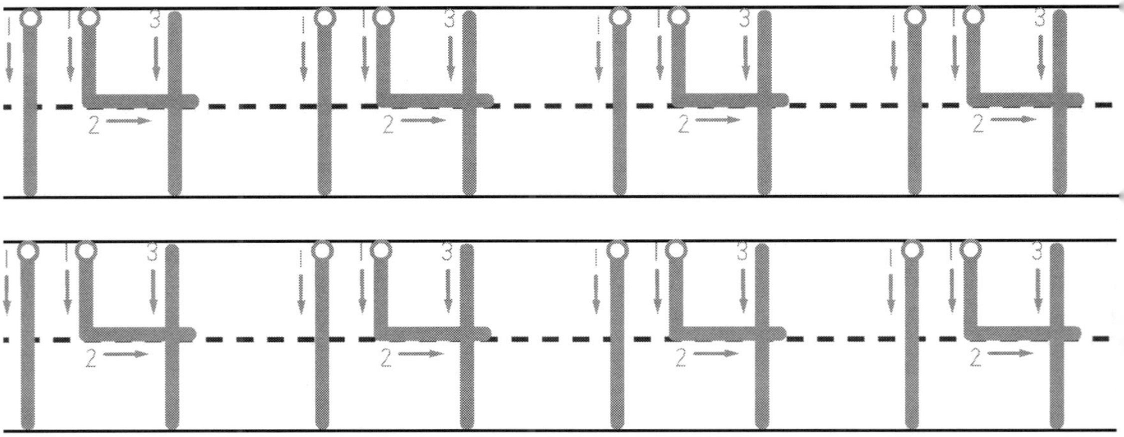

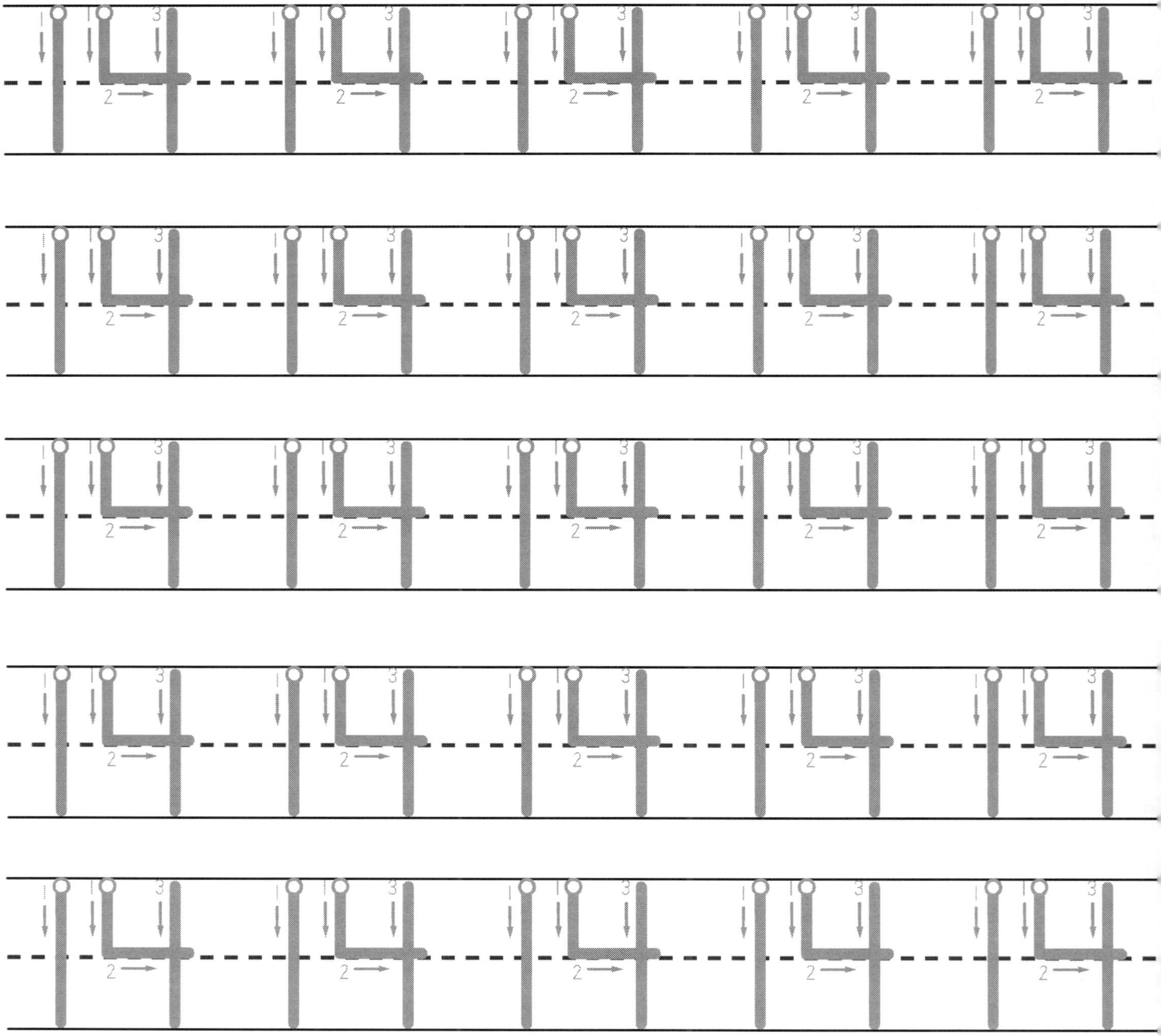

Penmanship Practice: Write 14

14

14

14

14

14

14

14

14

fourteen

Number Formation
with visual cues

Trace this number with your finger before beginning your writing lesson.

fifteen

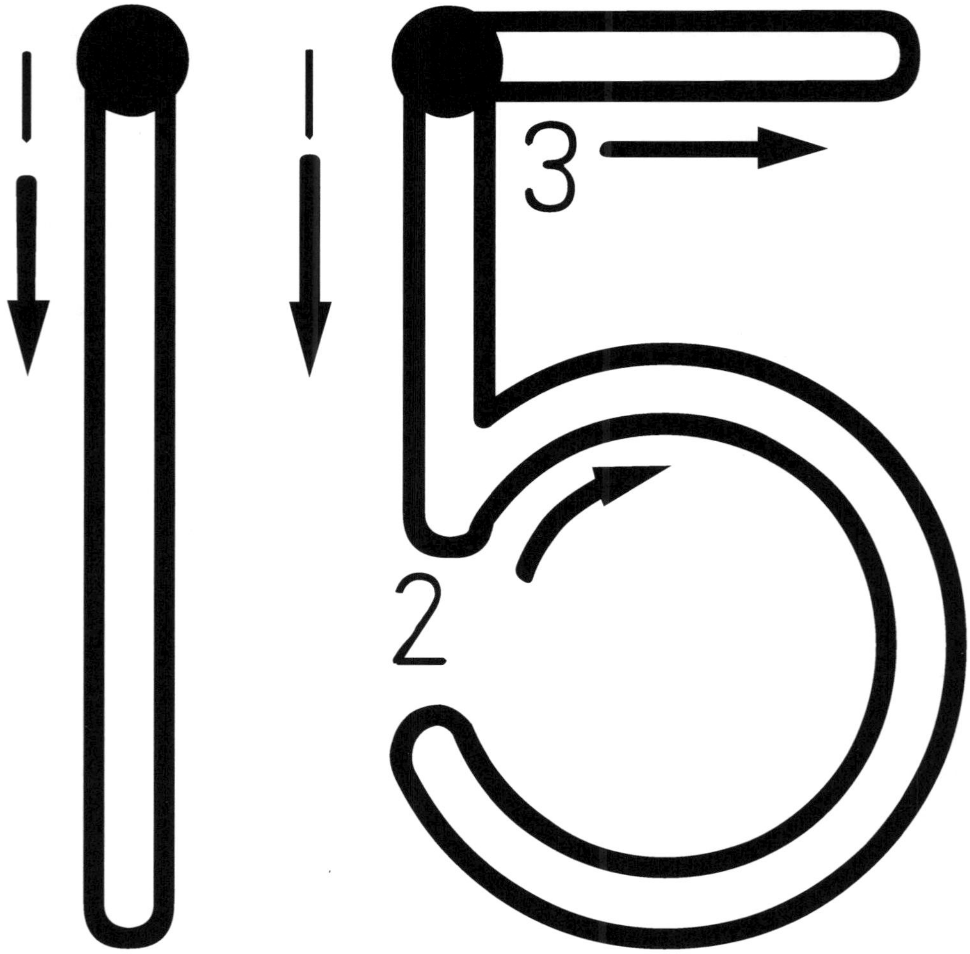

Fifteen can be written in no time,
First write 1, then write 5.

Count and Trace 15

Ants on a hill...

Fifteen little ants preparing winter's store,
One ant shouts, "We need one more!"

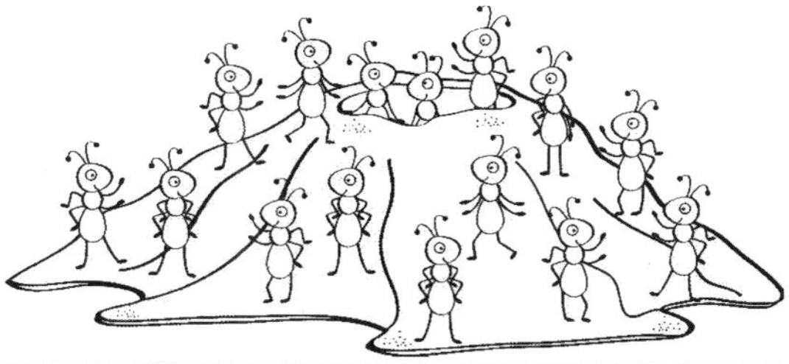

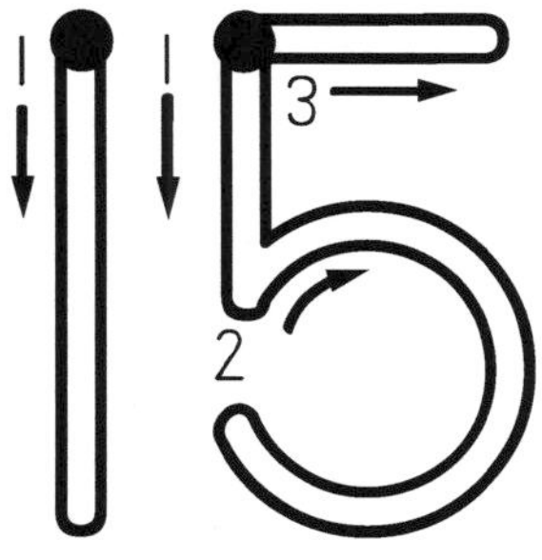

fifteen

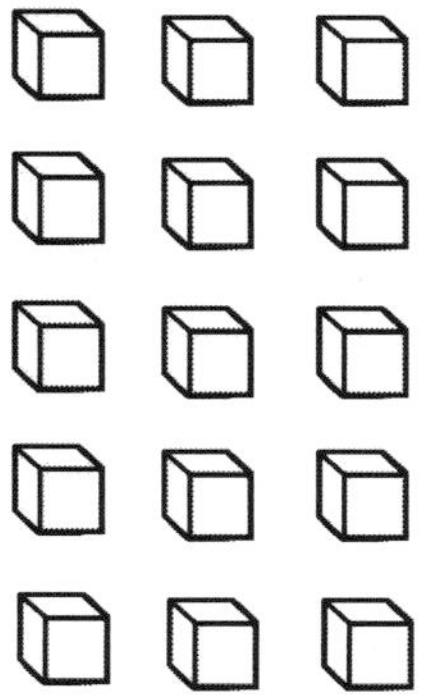

fifteen

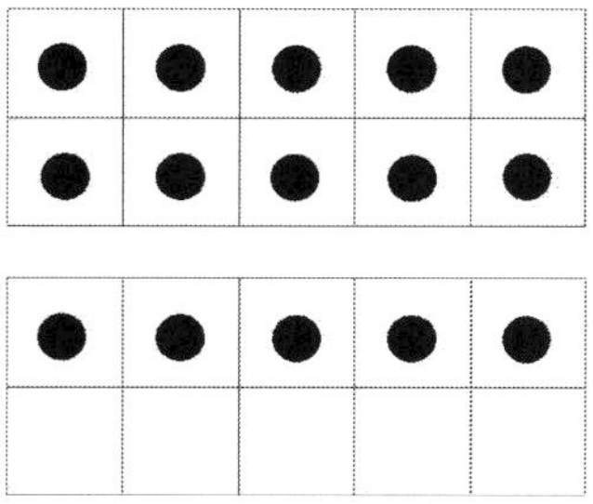

fifteen

Penmanship Practice: Trace 15

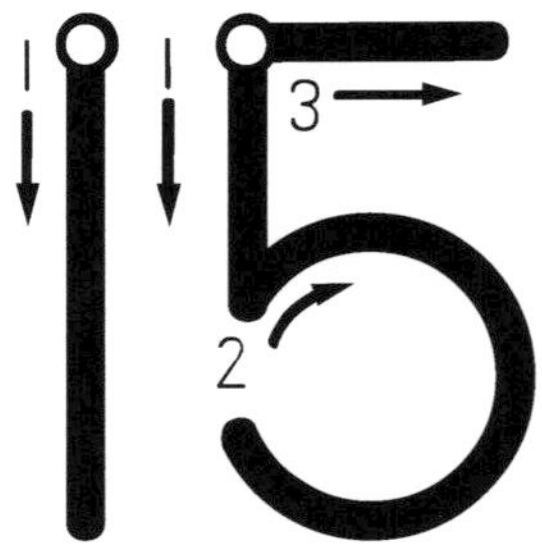

fifteen

Penmanship Practice: Write 15

15

15

15

15

15

15

15

1 1 2 3

15

fifteen

Number Formation
with visual cues

Trace this number with your finger before beginning your writing lesson.

sixteen

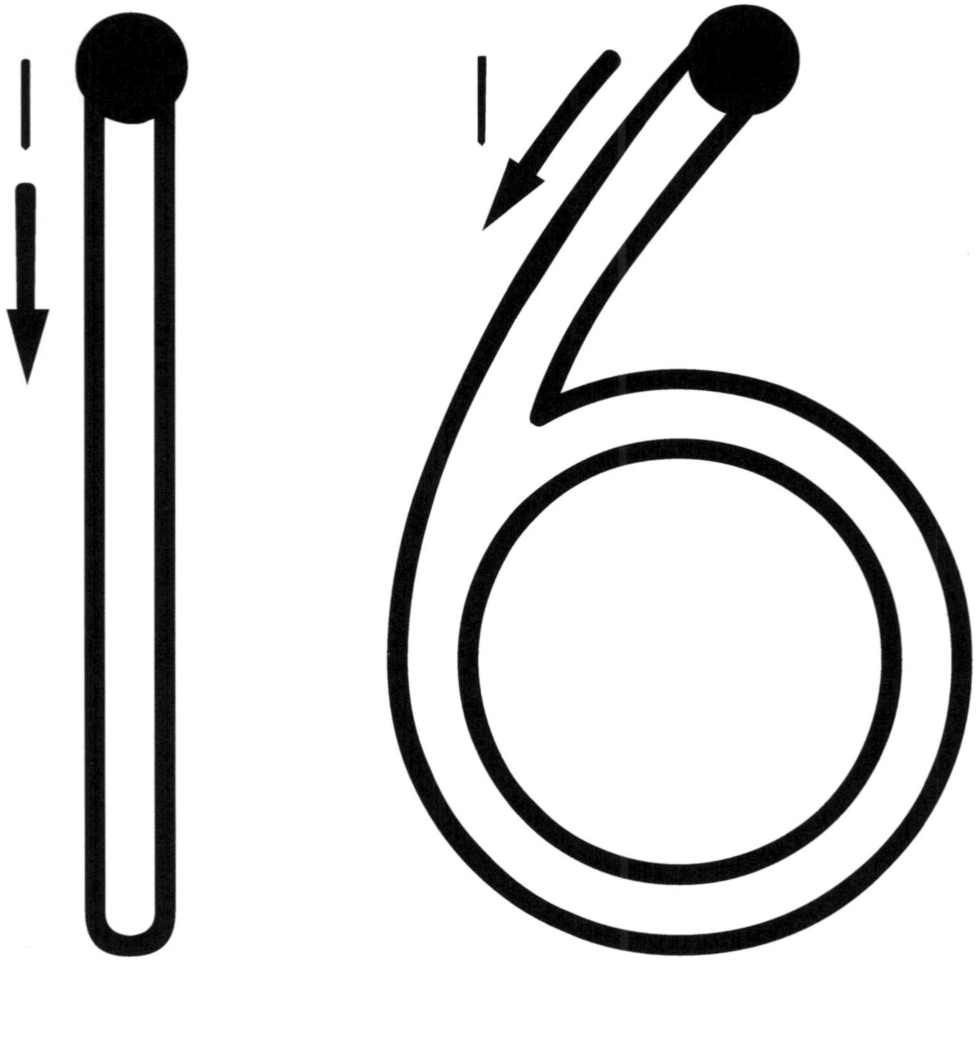

With sixteen there are no tricks,
Simply write a 1 and 6.

Count and Trace 16

Ants on a hill...

Sixteen little ants preparing winter's store,
One ant shouts, "We need one more!"

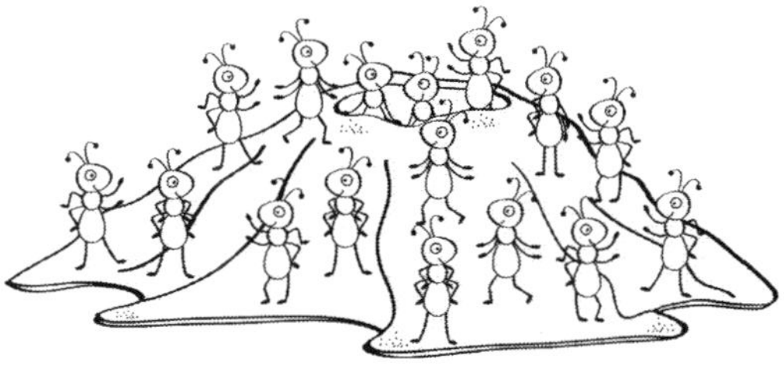

16

sixteen

16 16 16 16 16

16 16 16 16 16

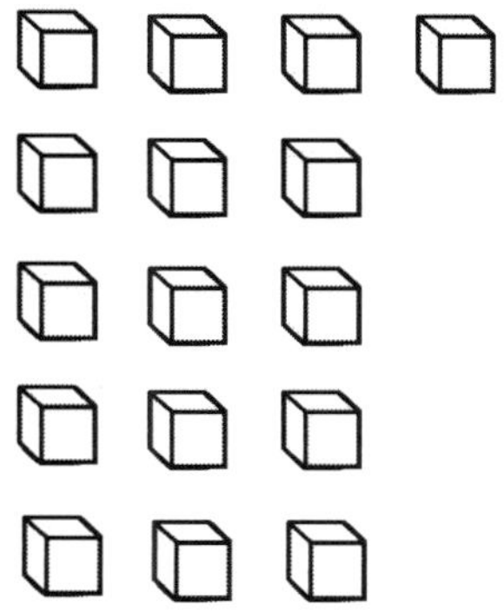

sixteen

16 16 16 16 16

16 16 16 16 16

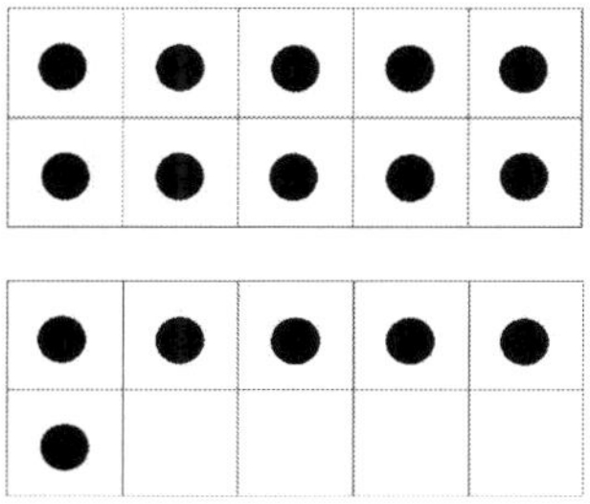

sixteen

16 16 16 16 16

16 16 16 16 16

Penmanship Practice: Trace 16

16
sixteen

16 16 16 16
16 16 16 16
16 16 16 16 16
16 16 16 16 16
16 16 16 16 16
16 16 16 16 16
16 16 16 16 16

Penmanship Practice: Write 16

16

16

16

16

16

16

16

16

sixteen

Number Formation
with visual cues

Trace this number with your finger before beginning your writing lesson.

seventeen

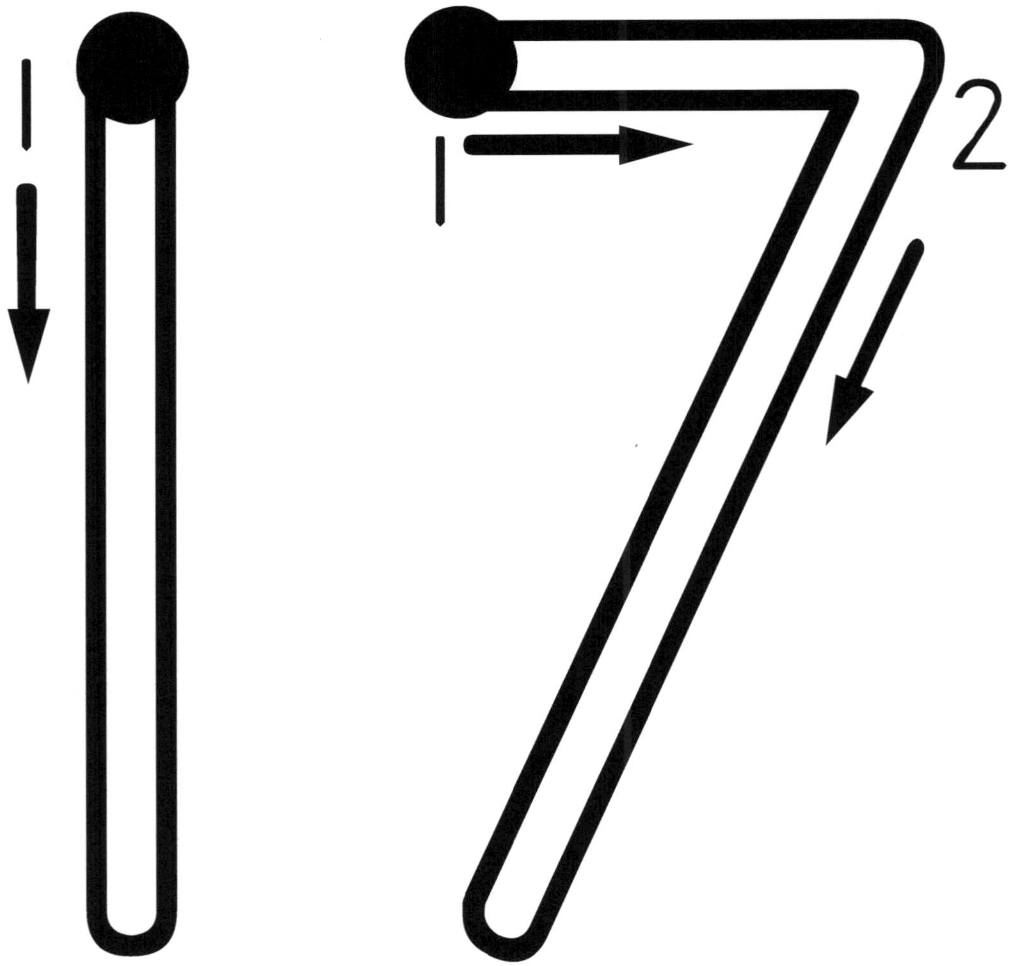

Here are two more numbers that we've seen,
1 and 7 make seventeen.

Count and Trace 17

Ants on a hill...

Seventeen little ants preparing winter's store,
One ant shouts, "We need one more!"

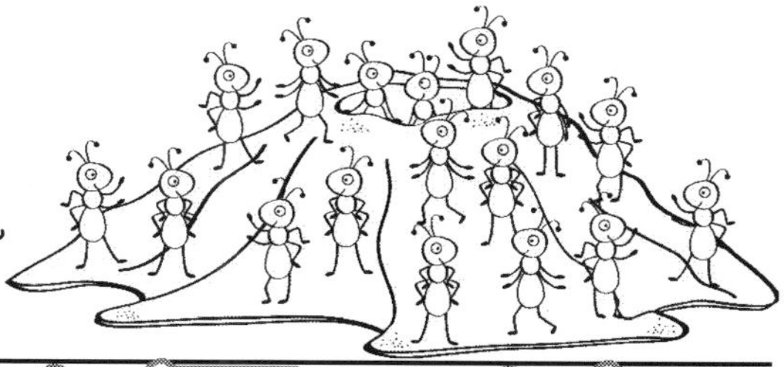

17

seventeen

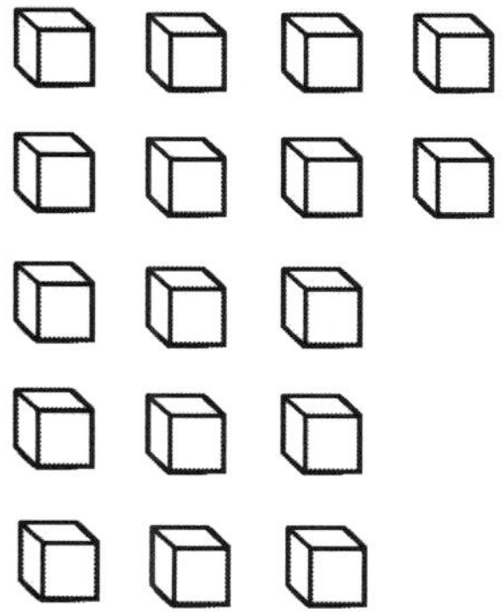

seventeen

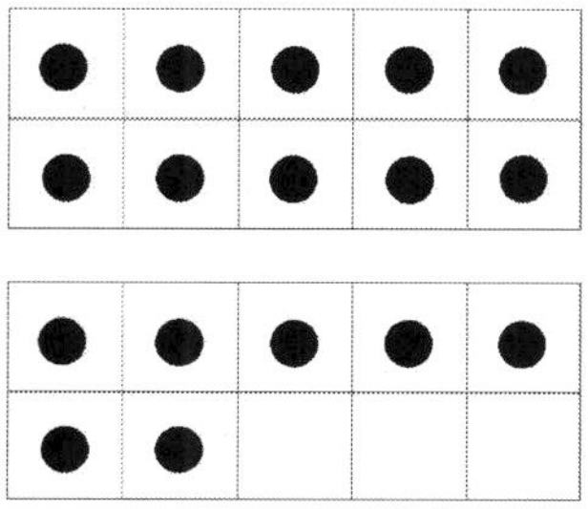

seventeen

Penmanship Practice: Trace 17

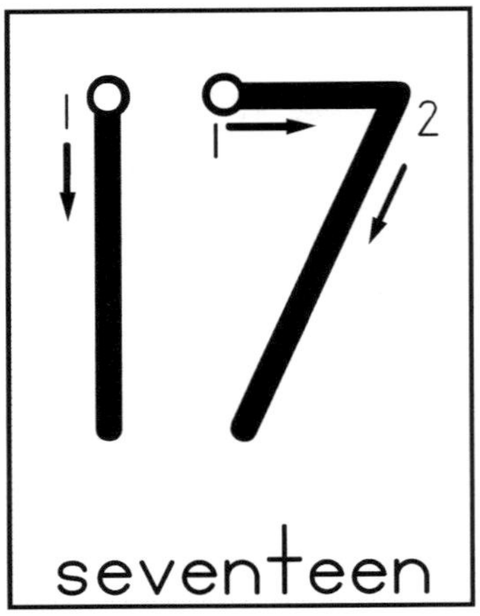

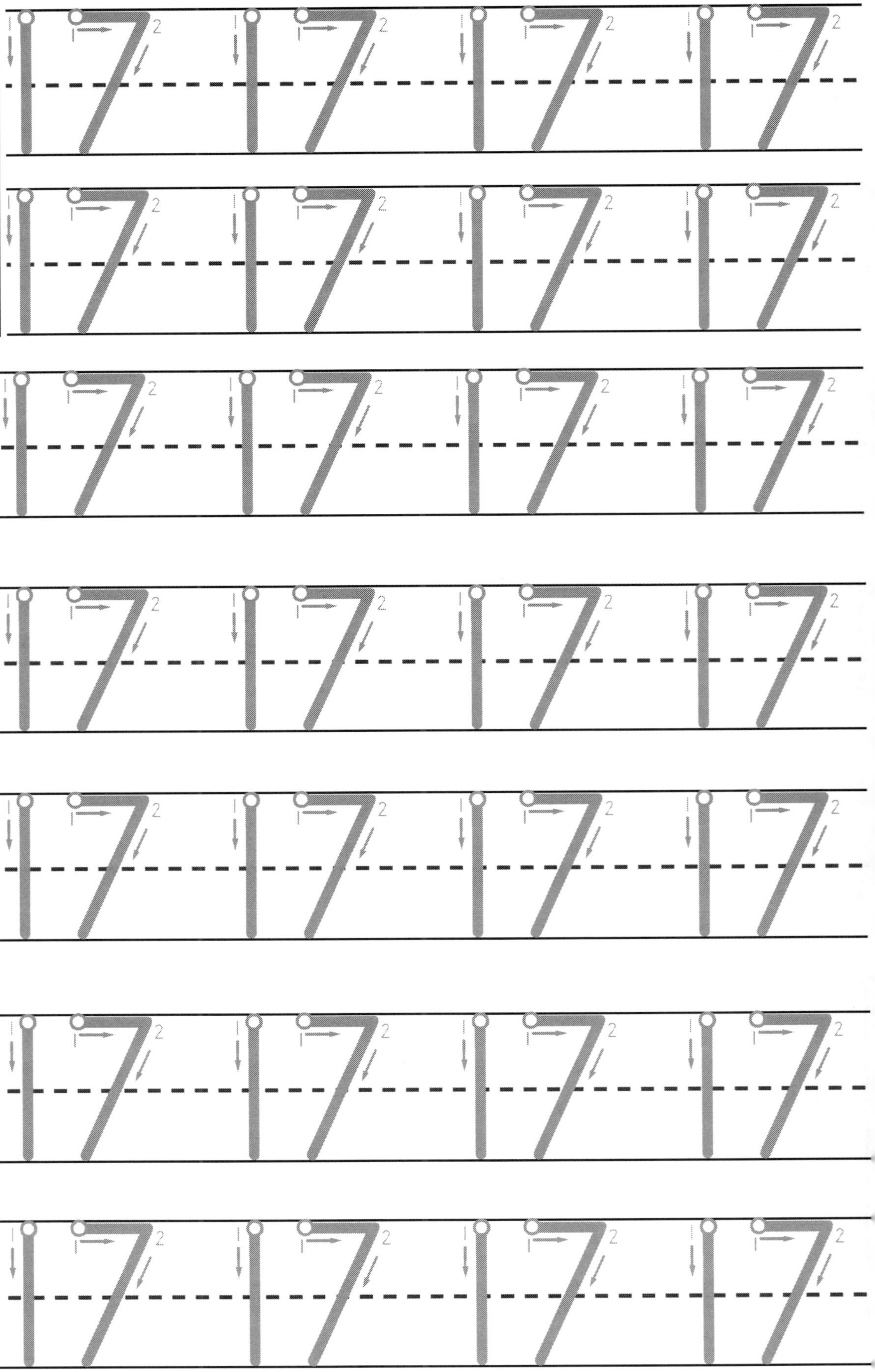

Penmanship Practice: Write 17

17

17

17

17

17

17

17

17

seventeen

Number Formation
with visual cues

Trace this number with your finger before beginning your writing lesson.

eighteen

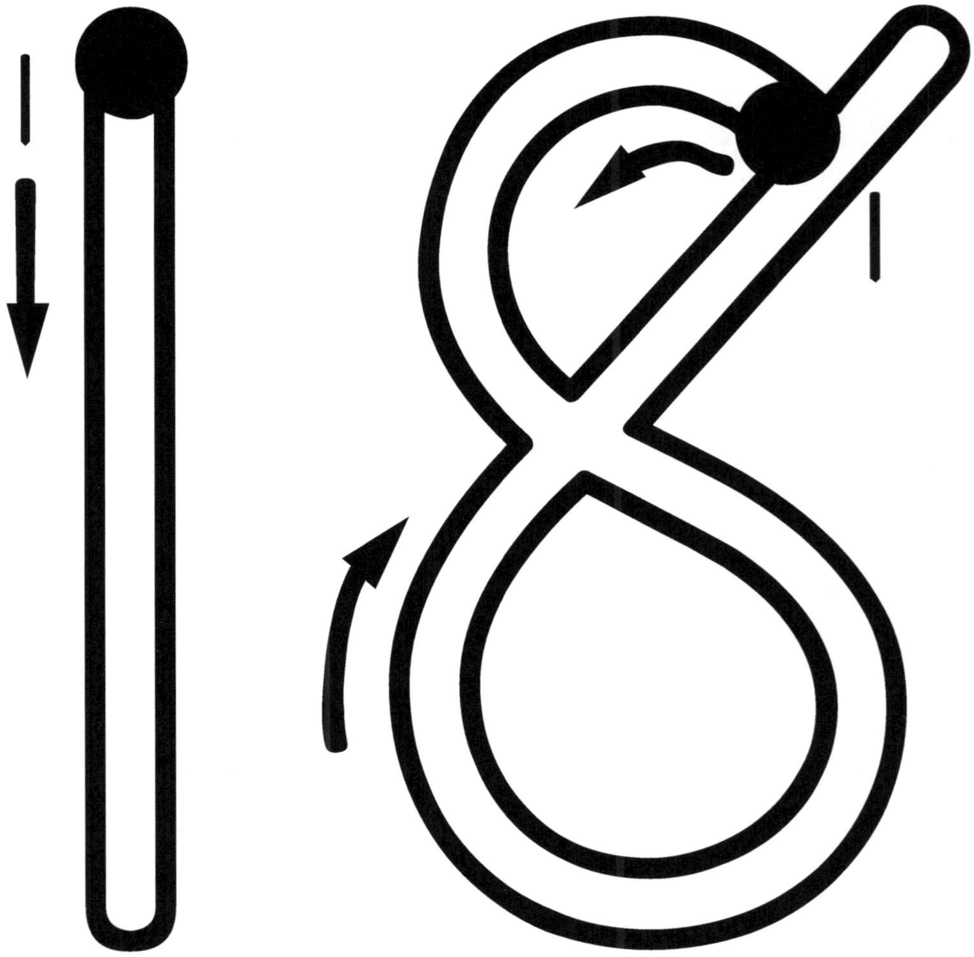

Eighteen, be sure and get it straight,
It's made up of a 1 and 8.

Count and Trace 18

Ants on a hill...

Eighteen little ants preparing winter's store,
One ant shouts, "We need one more!"

18

eighteen

18 18 18 18 18

18 18 18 18 18

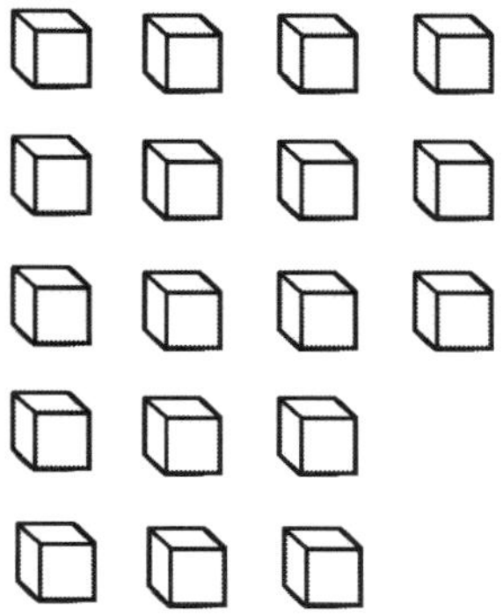

eighteen

18 18 18 18 18

18 18 18 18 18

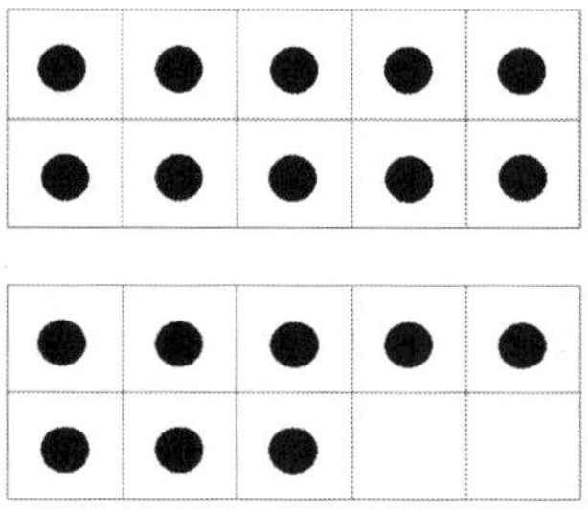

eighteen

18 18 18 18 18

18 18 18 18 18

Penmanship Practice: Trace 18

18

eighteen

18 18 18 18

18 18 18 18

18 18 18 18 18

18 18 18 18 18

18 18 18 18 18

18 18 18 18 18

18 18 18 18 18

Penmanship Practice: Write 18

18

18

18

18

18

18

18

18

eighteen

Number Formation

with visual cues

Trace this number with your finger before beginning your writing lesson.

nineteen

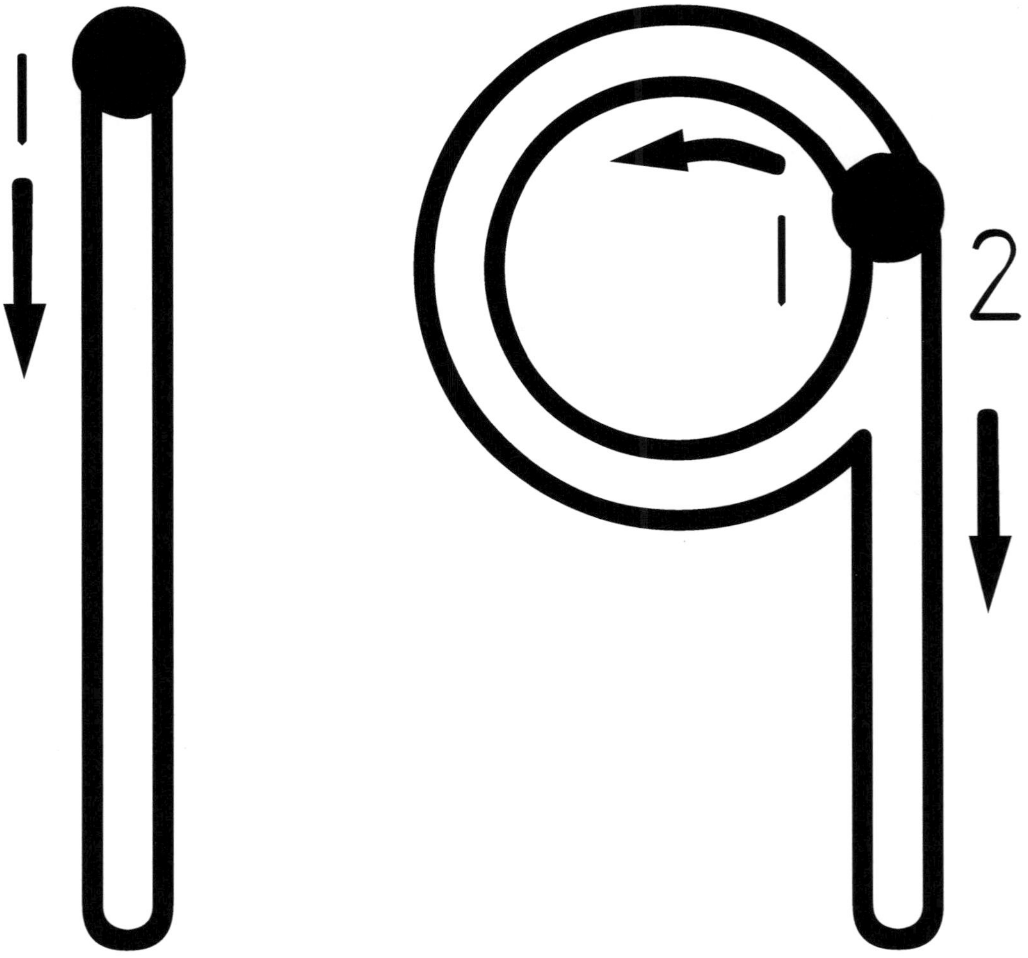

If I had a 1 and 9 in my hand,
I'd make nineteen, wouldn't that be grand?

Count and Trace 19

Ants on a hill...

Nineteen little ants preparing winter's store,
One ant shouts, "We need one more!"

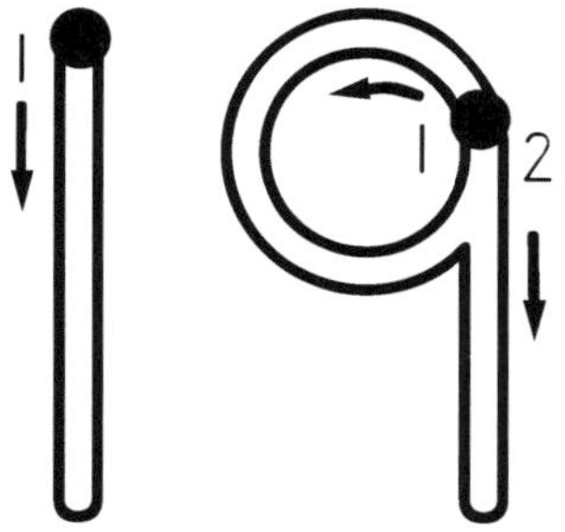

nineteen

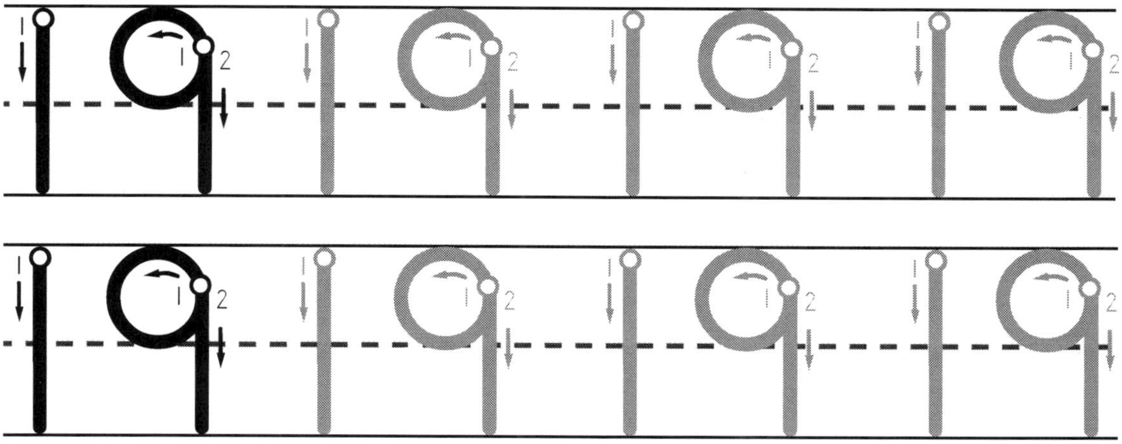

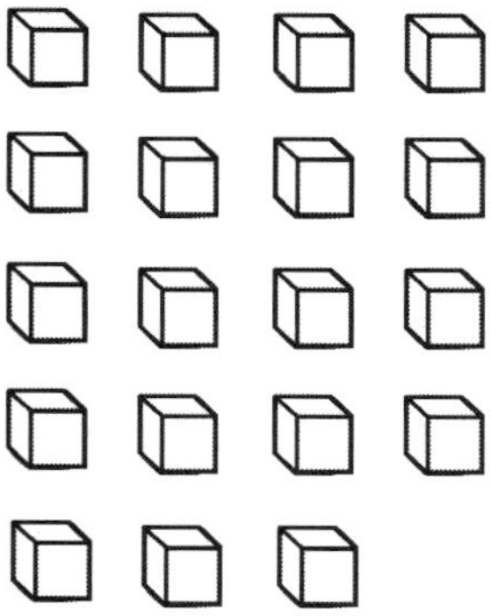

nineteen

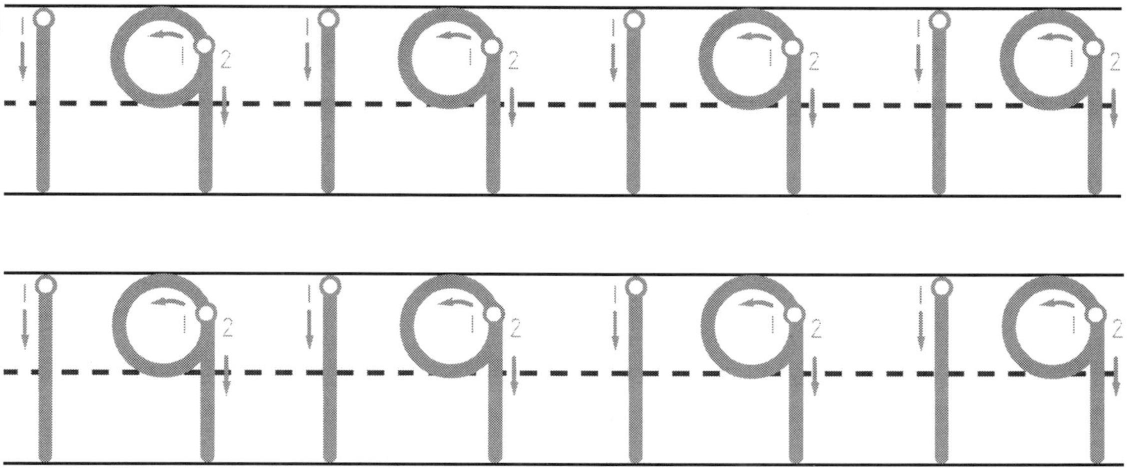

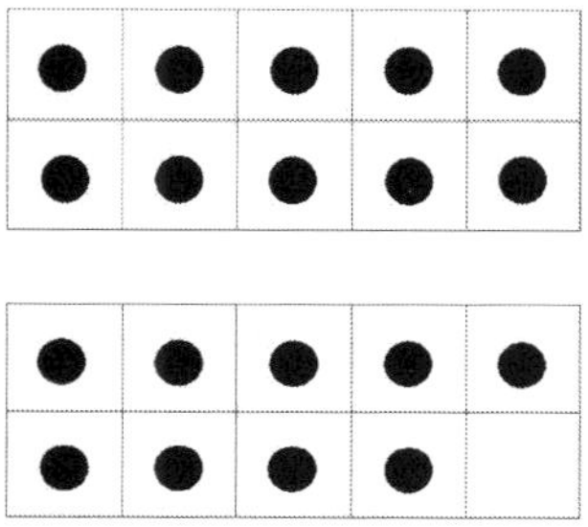

nineteen

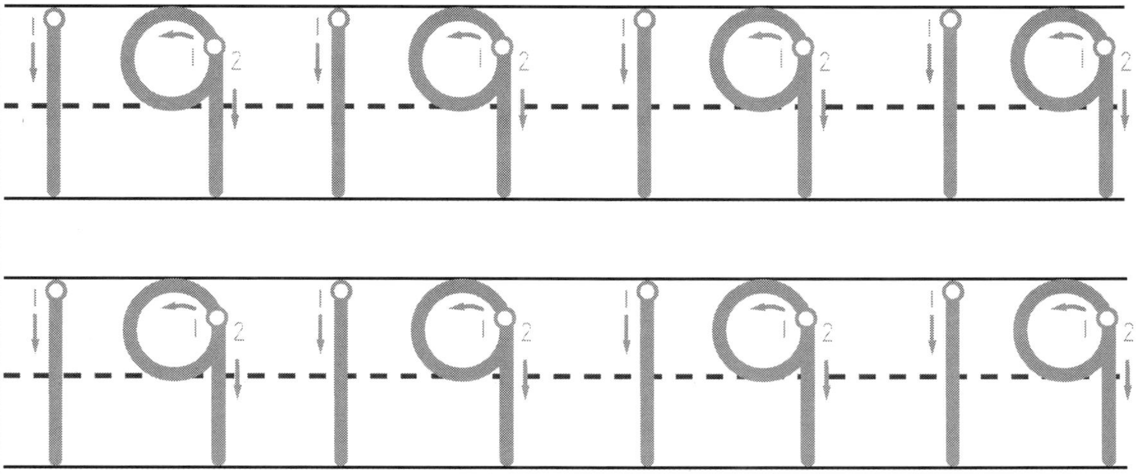

Penmanship Practice: Trace 19

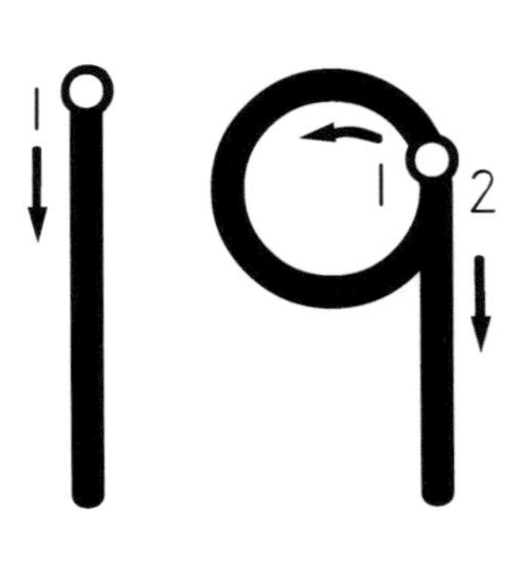

nineteen

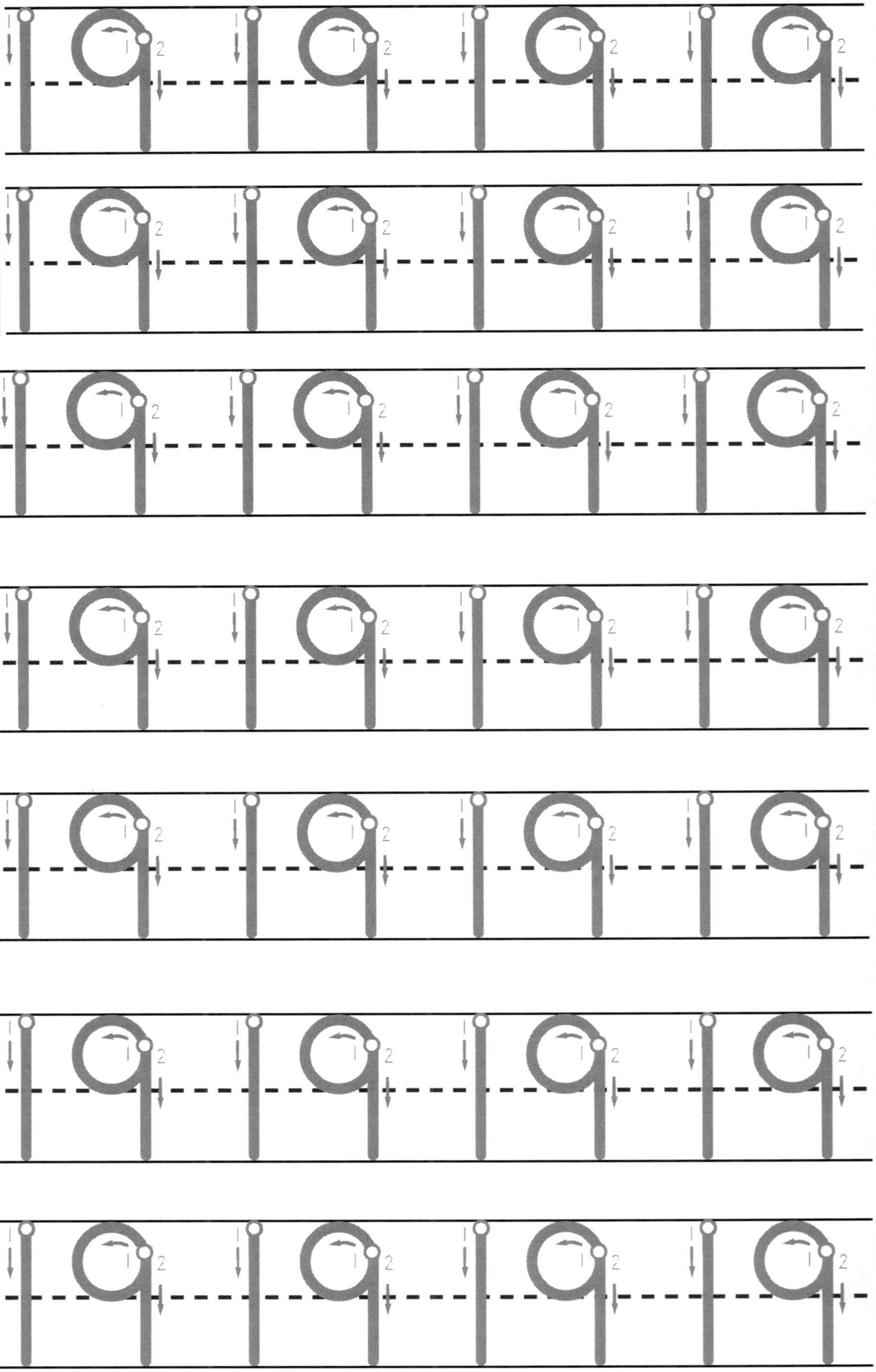

Penmanship Practice: Write 19

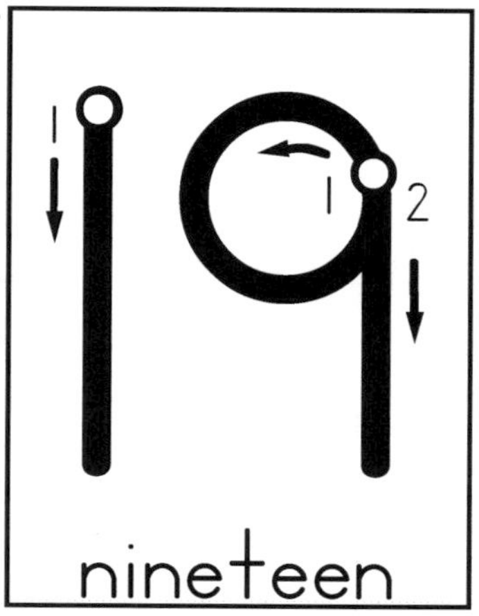

Number Formation
with visual cues

Trace this number with your finger before beginning your writing lesson.

twenty

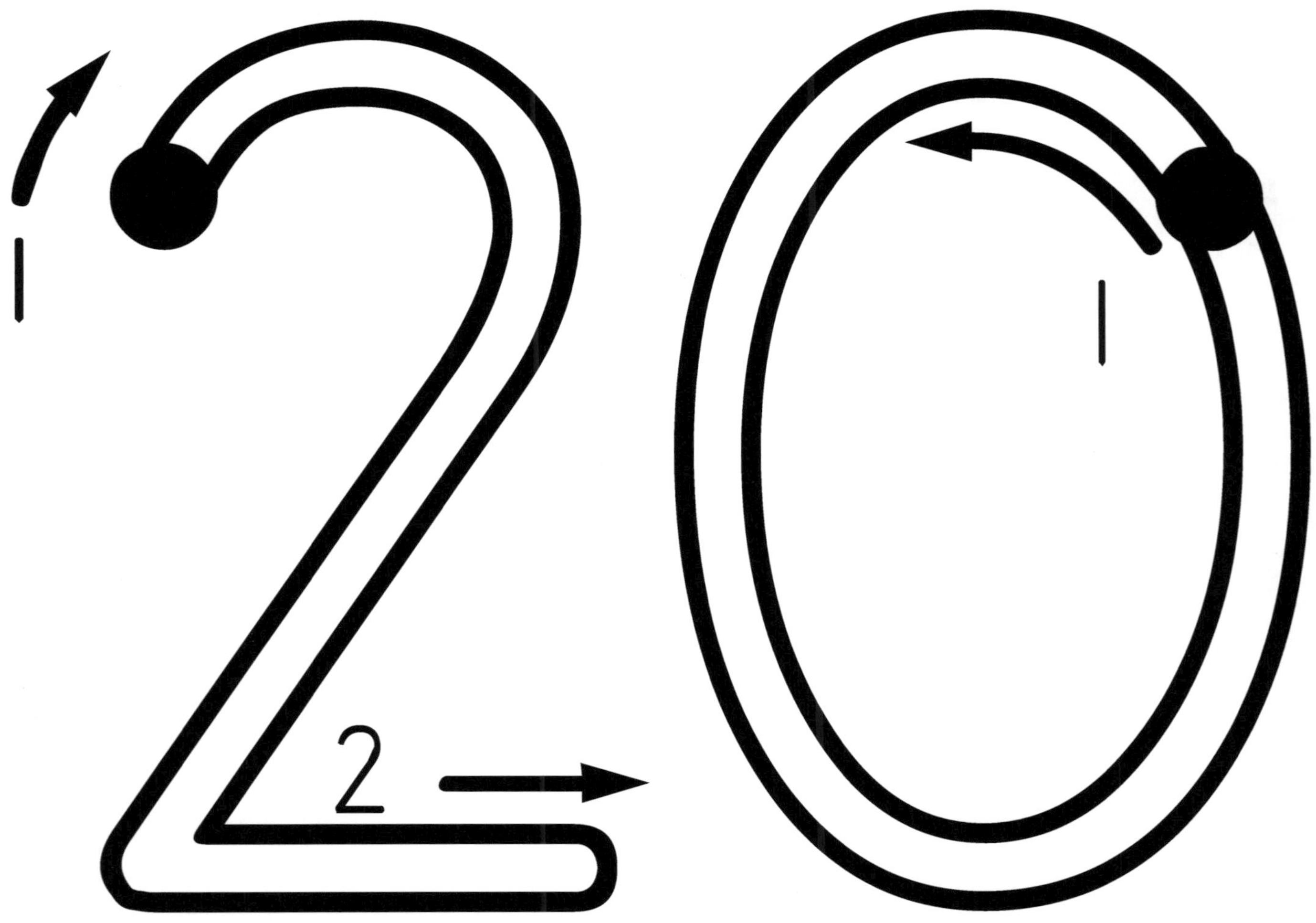

We've reached twenty! Let's end here,
With 2 and 0, our last number pair.

Count and Trace 20

Ants on a hill...

Twenty little ants preparing winter's store,
One ant shouts, "Please, no more!"

20

twenty

20 20 20

20 20 20

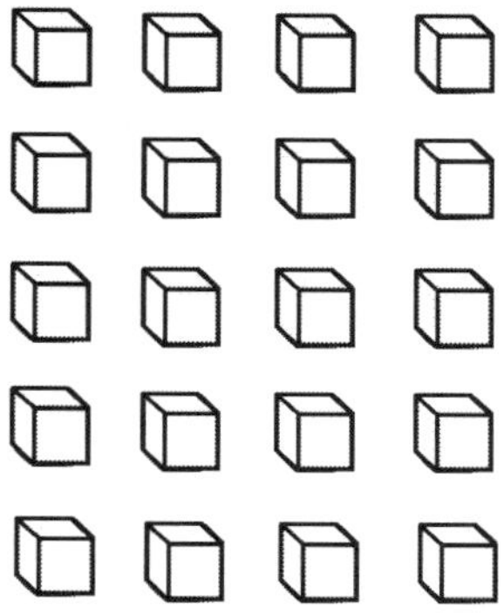

twenty

20 20 20

20 20 20

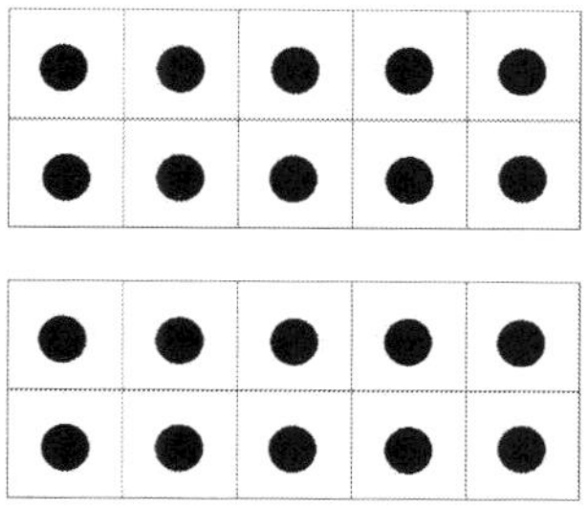

twenty

20 20 20

20 20 20

Penmanship Practice: Trace 20

20

twenty

20 20 20

20 20 20

20 20 20 20

20 20 20 20

20 20 20 20

20 20 20 20

20 20 20 20

Penmanship Practice: Write 20

20

20

20

20

20

20

20

20

twenty

Busy Bees Practice Review

0 little busy bees leaving the hive. . .

How many do you think there are inside?

0

zero

0

0

0

0

Busy Bees Practice Review

1 little busy bee leaving the hive. . .

How many do you think there are left inside?

1

one

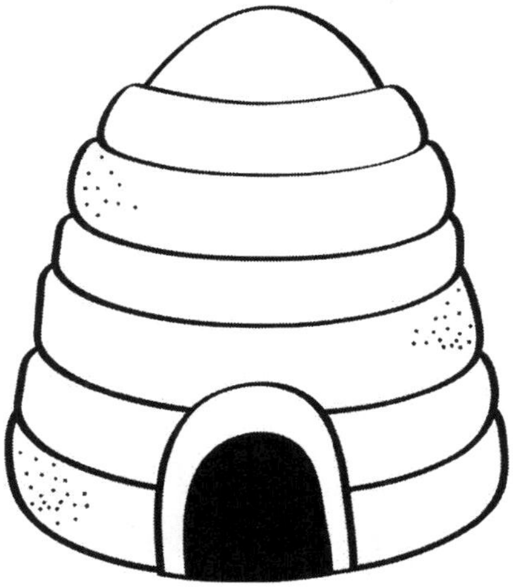

Busy Bees Practice Review

2 little busy bees leaving the hive. . .

How many do you think there are left inside?

2

two

2

2

2

2

Busy Bees Practice Review

3 little busy bees leaving the hive...

How many do you think there are left inside?

3

three

3

3

3

3

Busy Bees Practice Review

4 little busy bees leaving the hive. . .

How many do you think there are left inside?

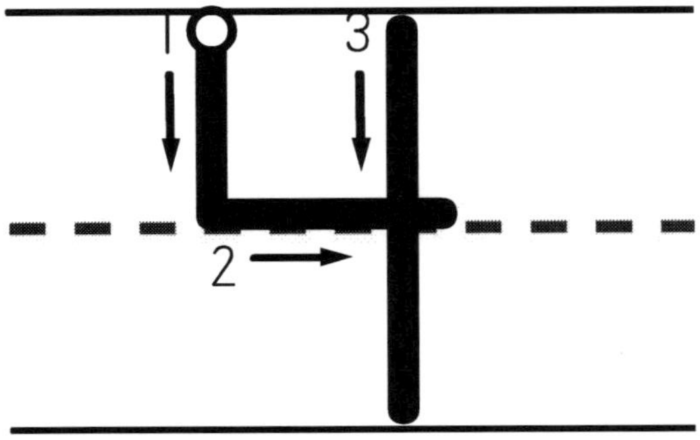

four

Busy Bees Practice Review

5 little busy bees leaving the hive. . .

How many do you think there are left inside?

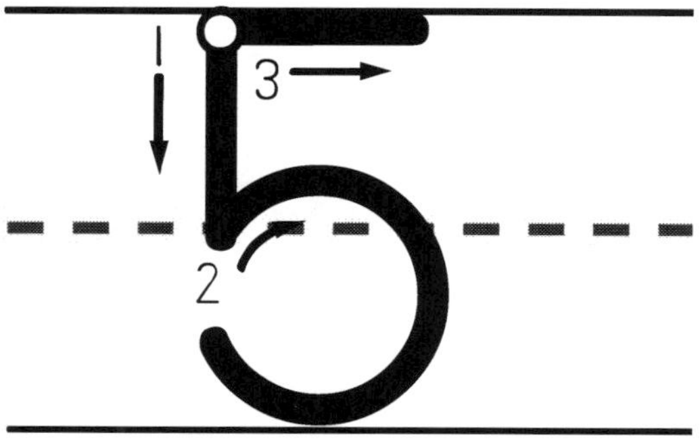

five

5

5

5

5

Busy Bees Practice Review

6 little busy bees leaving the hive. . .

How many do you think there are left inside?

6

six

6

6

6

6

Busy Bees Practice Review

7 little busy bees leaving the hive. . .

How many do you think there are left inside?

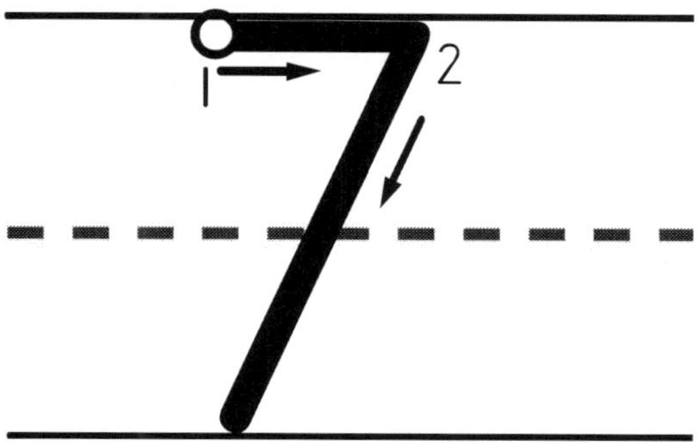

seven

Busy Bees Practice Review

8 little busy bees leaving the hive. . .

How many do you think there are left inside?

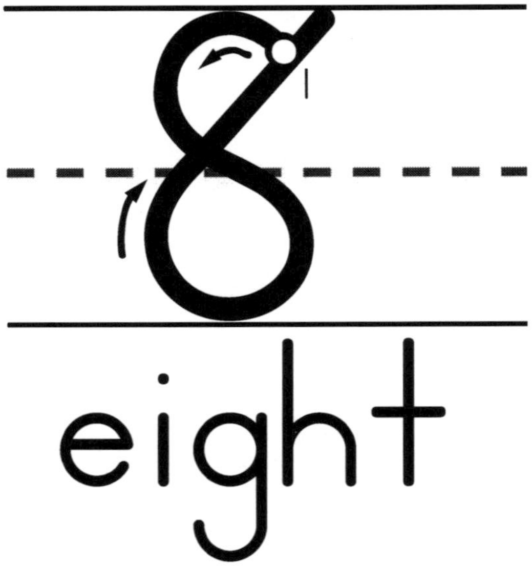

Busy Bees Practice Review

9 little busy bees leaving the hive...

How many do you think there are left inside?

9

nine

9

9

9

9

Busy Bees Practice Review

10 little busy bees leaving the hive. . .

How many do you think there are left inside?

10

ten

10

10

10

10

Busy Bees Practice Review

11 little busy bees leaving the hive. . .

How many do you think there are left inside?

11

eleven

Busy Bees Practice Review

12 little busy bees leaving the hive. . .

How many do you think there are left inside?

12

twelve

12

12

12

12

Busy Bees Practice Review

13 little busy bees leaving the hive. . .

How many do you think there are left inside?

13

thirteen

13

13

13

13

Busy Bees Practice Review

14 little busy bees leaving the hive. . .

How many do you think there are left inside?

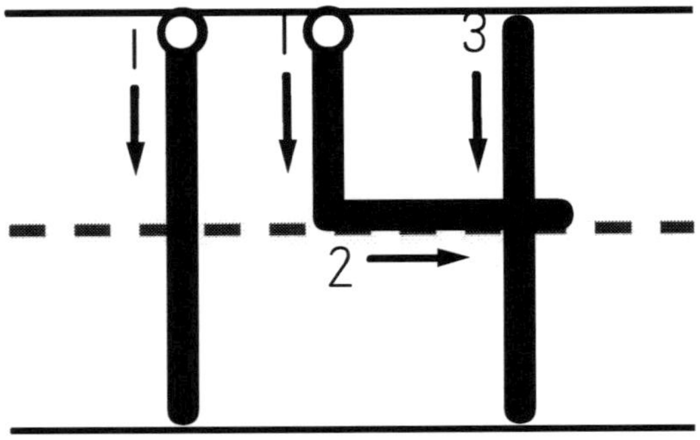

fourteen

14

14

14

14

Busy Bees Practice Review

15 little busy bees leaving the hive. . .

How many do you think there are left inside?

15

fifteen

15

15

15

15

Busy Bees Practice Review

16 little busy bees leaving the hive. . .

How many do you think there are left inside?

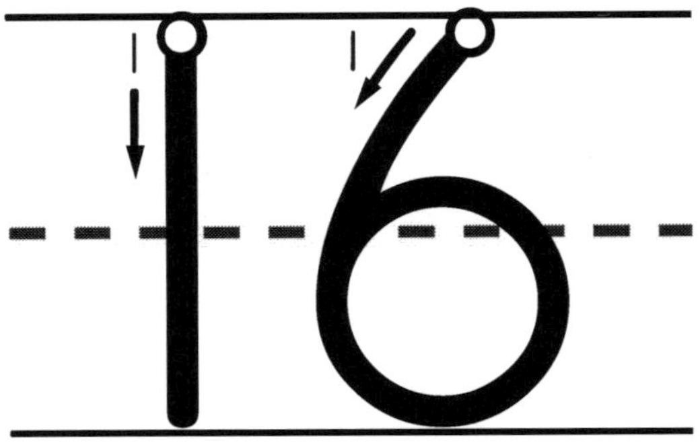

sixteen

16

16

16

16

Busy Bees Practice Review

17 little busy bees leaving the hive. . .

How many do you think there are left inside?

17

seventeen

17

17

17

17

Busy Bees Practice Review

18 little busy bees leaving the hive. . .

How many do you think there are left inside?

18

eighteen

18

18

18

18

Busy Bees Practice Review

19 little busy bees leaving the hive...

How many do you think there are left inside?

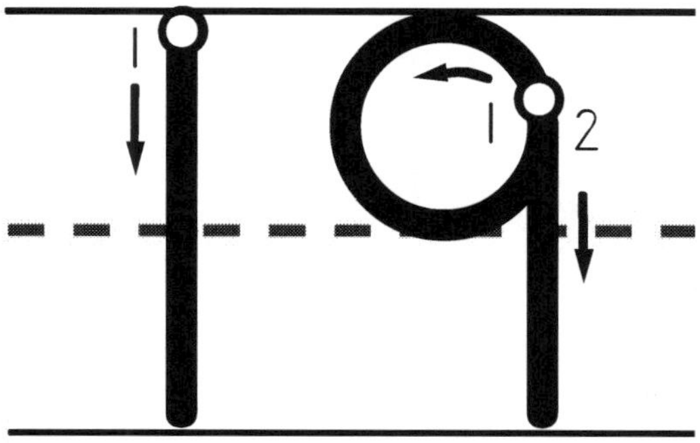

nineteen

19

19

19

19

Busy Bees Practice Review

20 little busy bees buzzing toward the hive. . .

They've ended their day and are heading inside.

20

20

20

20

Manipulative Workmat

Use this manipulative workmat to reinforce how each number is formed.

zero

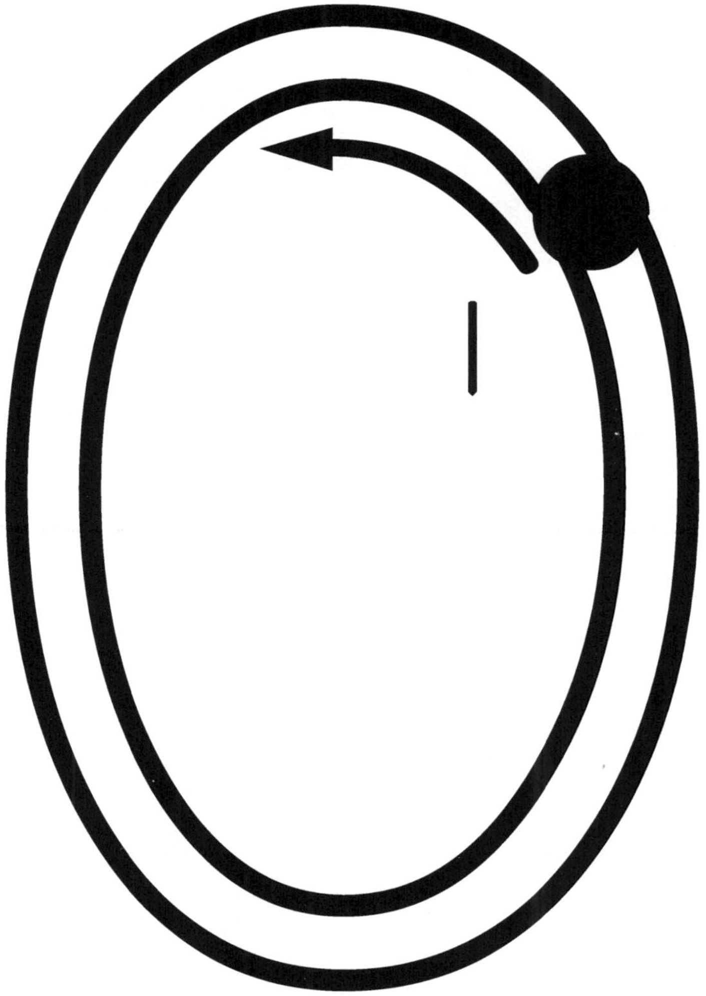

Cut along this line. Laminate or copy for extended use.

Manipulative Workmat

Use this manipulative workmat to reinforce how each number is formed.

one

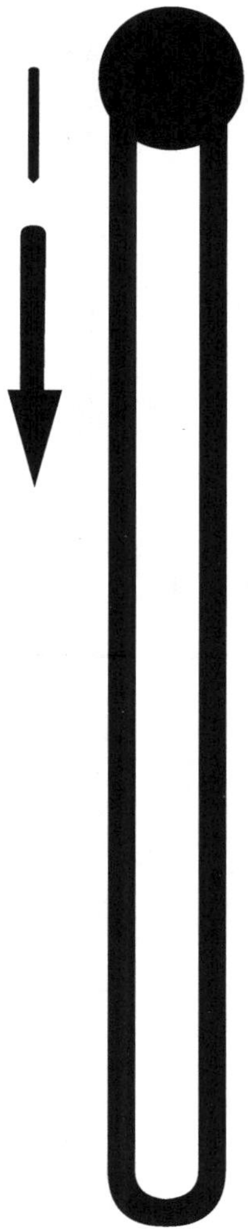

Cut along this line. Laminate or copy for extended use.

Manipulative Workmat

Use this manipulative workmat to reinforce how each number is formed.

two

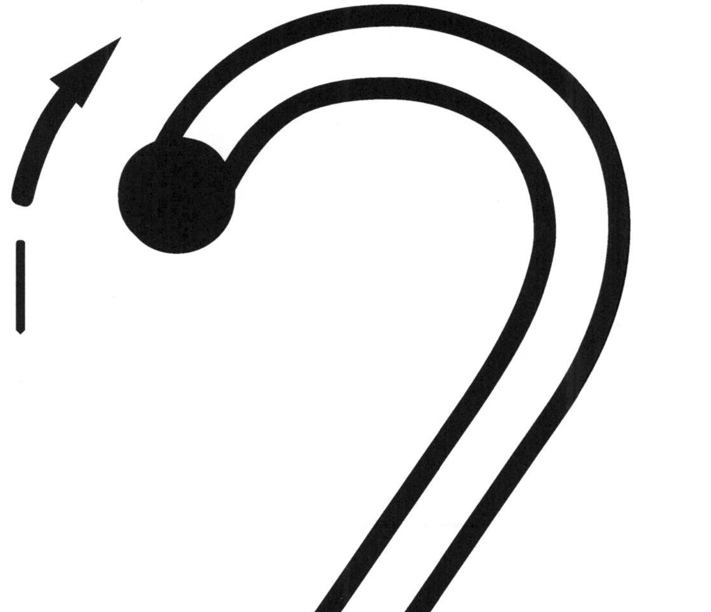

Cut along this line. Laminate or copy for extended use.

Manipulative Workmat

Use this manipulative workmat to reinforce how each number is formed.

three

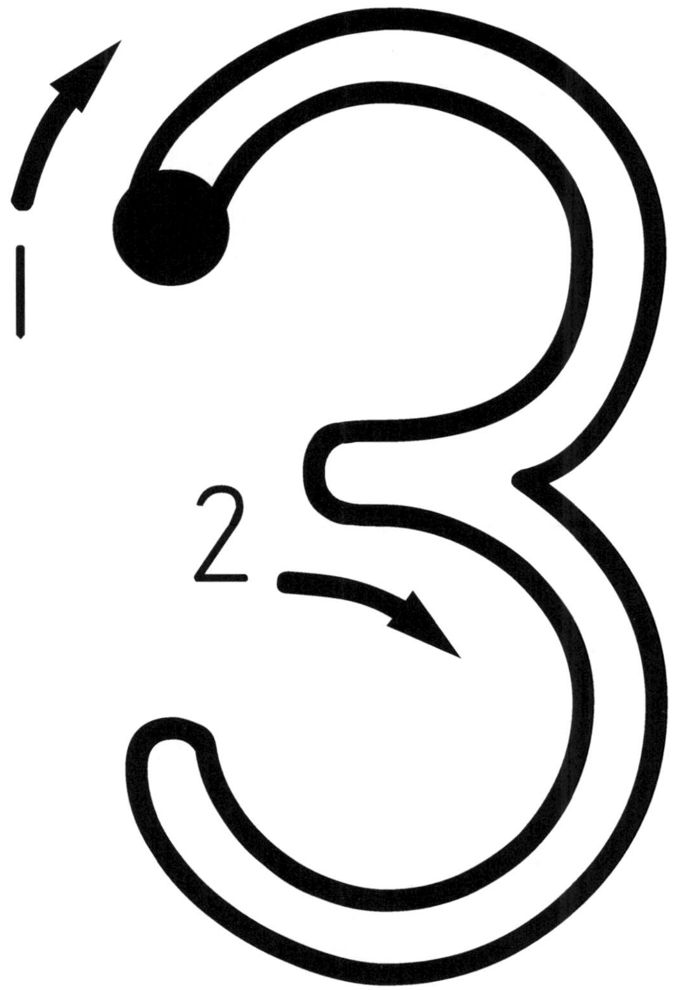

Cut along this line. Laminate or copy for extended use.

Cut along this line. Laminate or copy for extended use.

Manipulative Workmat

Use this manipulative workmat to reinforce how each number is formed.

four

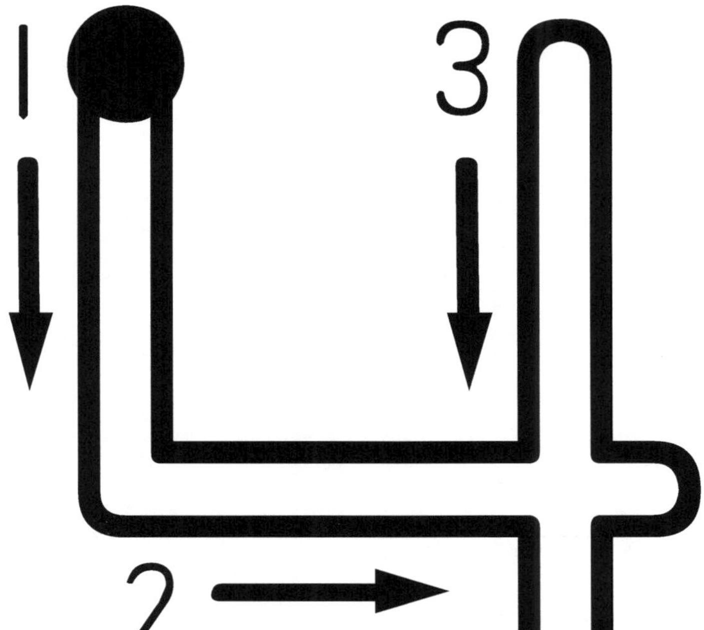

Manipulative Workmat

Use this manipulative workmat to reinforce how each number is formed.

five

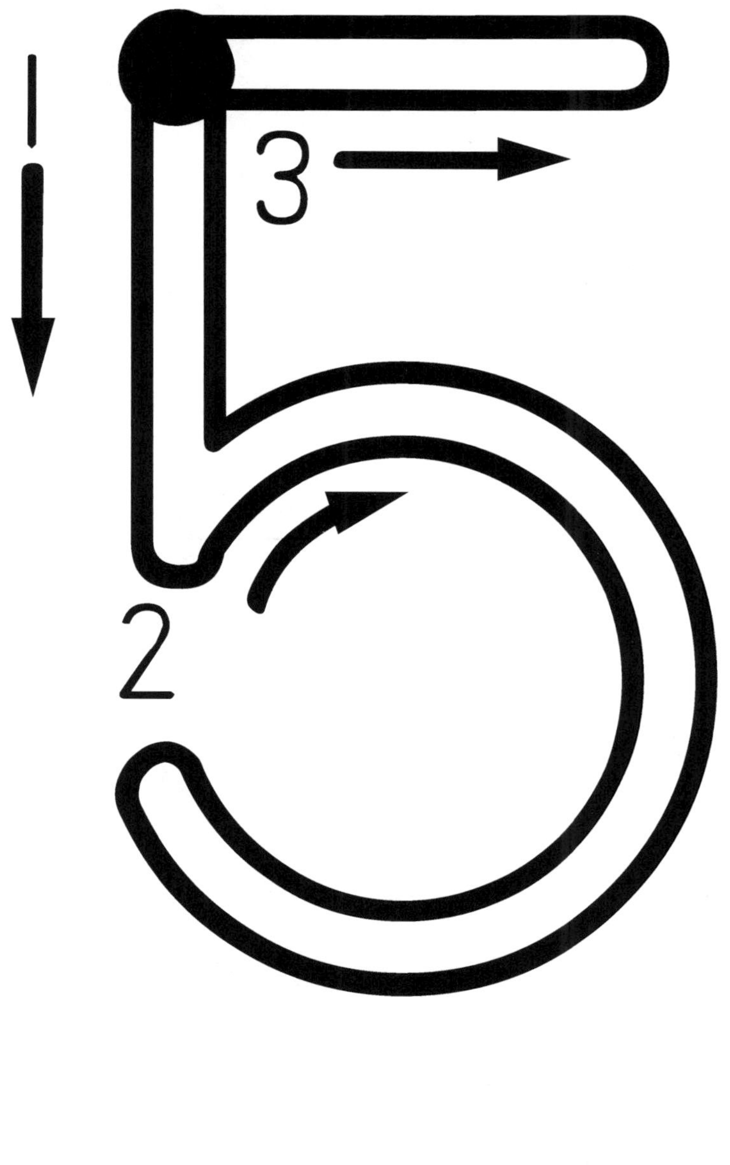

Cut along this line. Laminate or copy for extended use.

Manipulative Workmat

Use this manipulative workmat to reinforce how each number is formed.

six

Cut along this line. Laminate or copy for extended use.

Cut along this line. Laminate or copy for extended use.

Manipulative Workmat

Use this manipulative workmat to reinforce how each number is formed.

seven

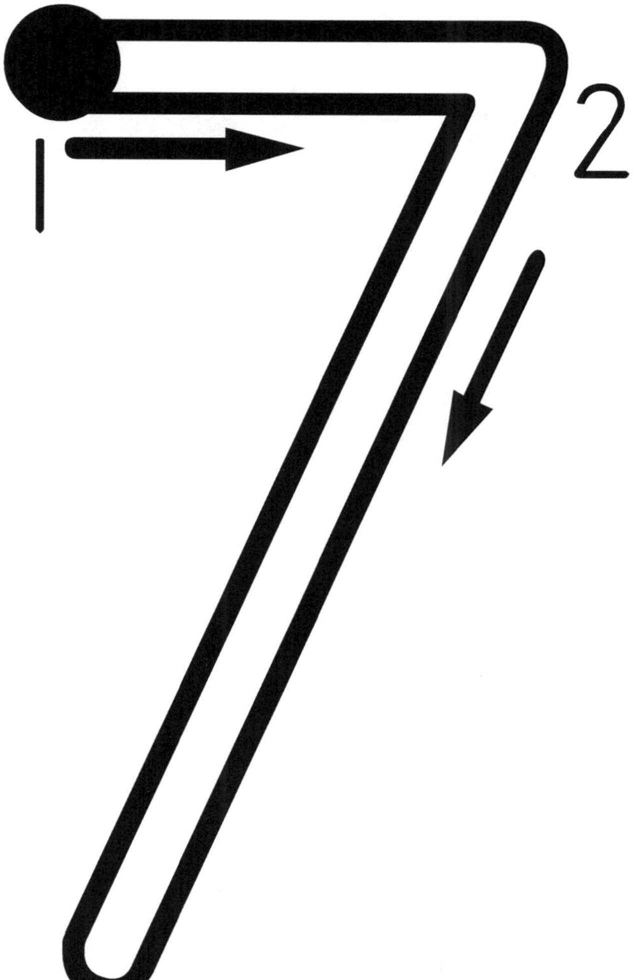

Manipulative Workmat

Use this manipulative workmat to reinforce how each number is formed.

eight

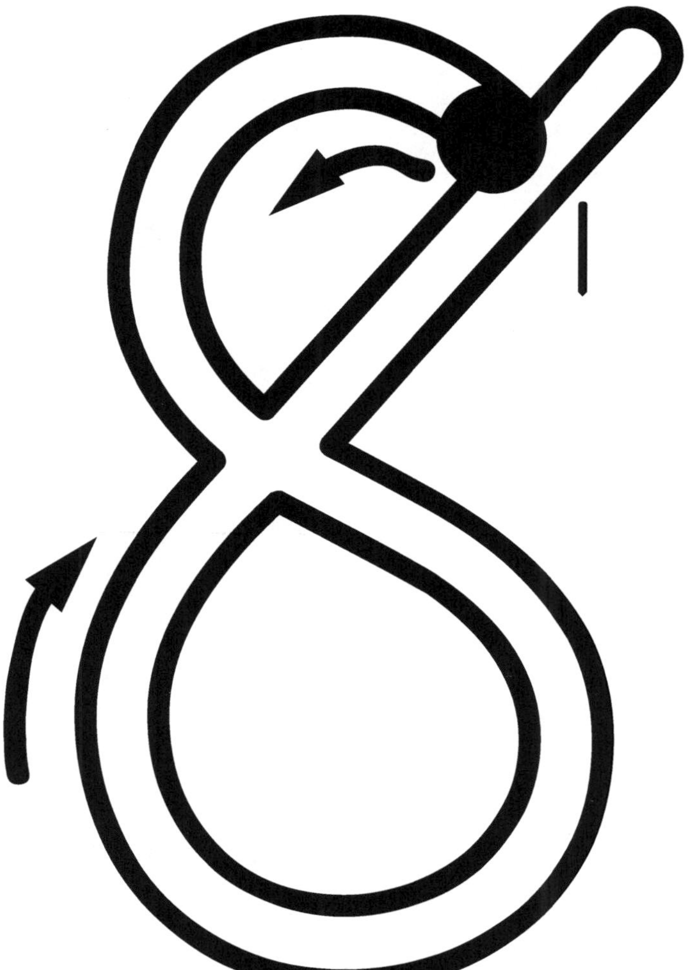

Cut along this line. Laminate or copy for extended use.

Cut along this line. Laminate or copy for extended use.

Manipulative Workmat

Use this manipulative workmat to reinforce how each number is formed.

nine

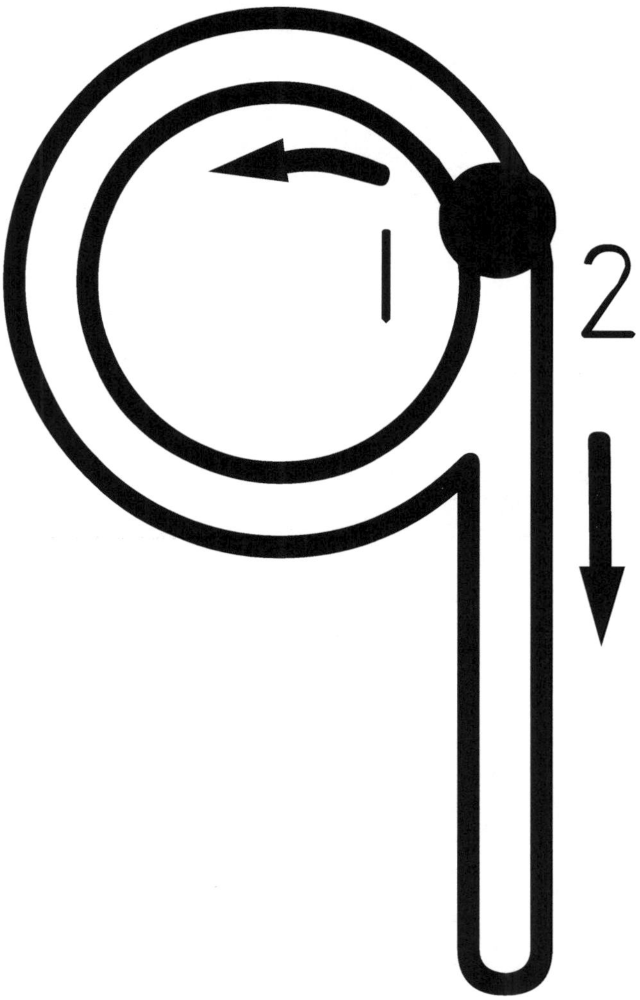

Manipulative Workmat

Use this manipulative workmat to reinforce how each number is formed.

ten

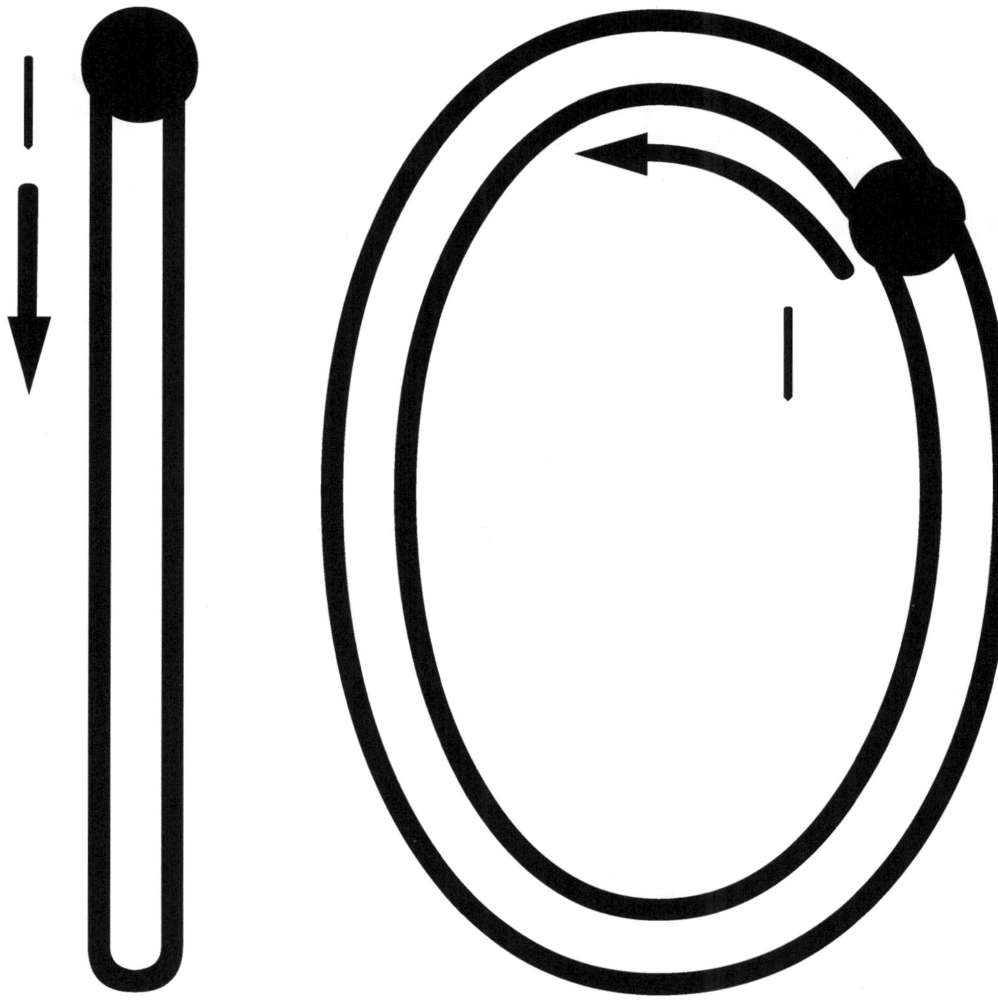

Cut along this line. Laminate or copy for extended use.

Manipulative Workmat

Use this manipulative workmat to reinforce how each number is formed.

eleven

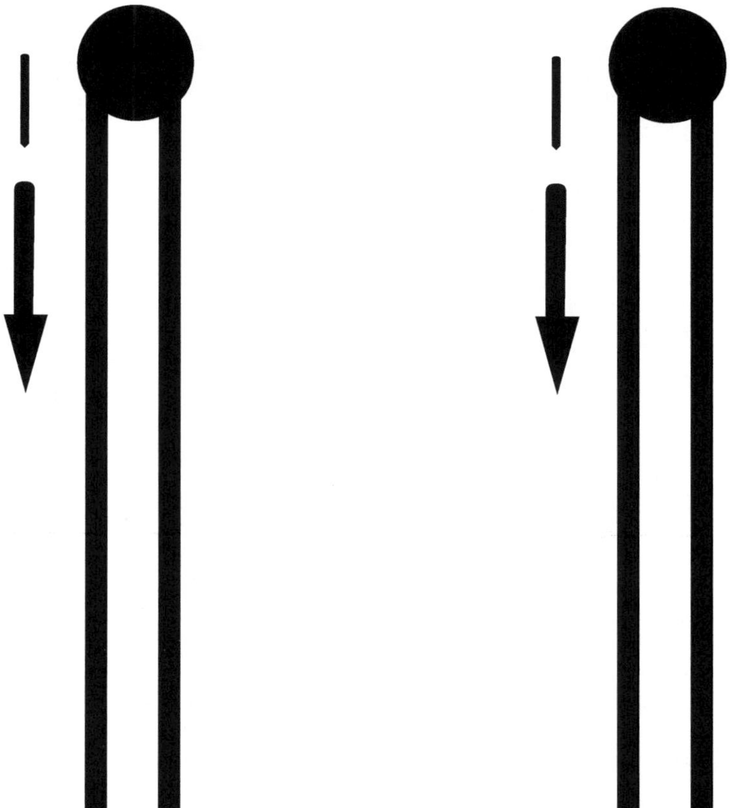

Cut along this line. Laminate or copy for extended use.

Manipulative Workmat

Use this manipulative workmat to reinforce how each number is formed.

twelve

Cut along this line. Laminate or copy for extended use.

Manipulative Workmat

Use this manipulative workmat to reinforce how each number is formed.

thirteen

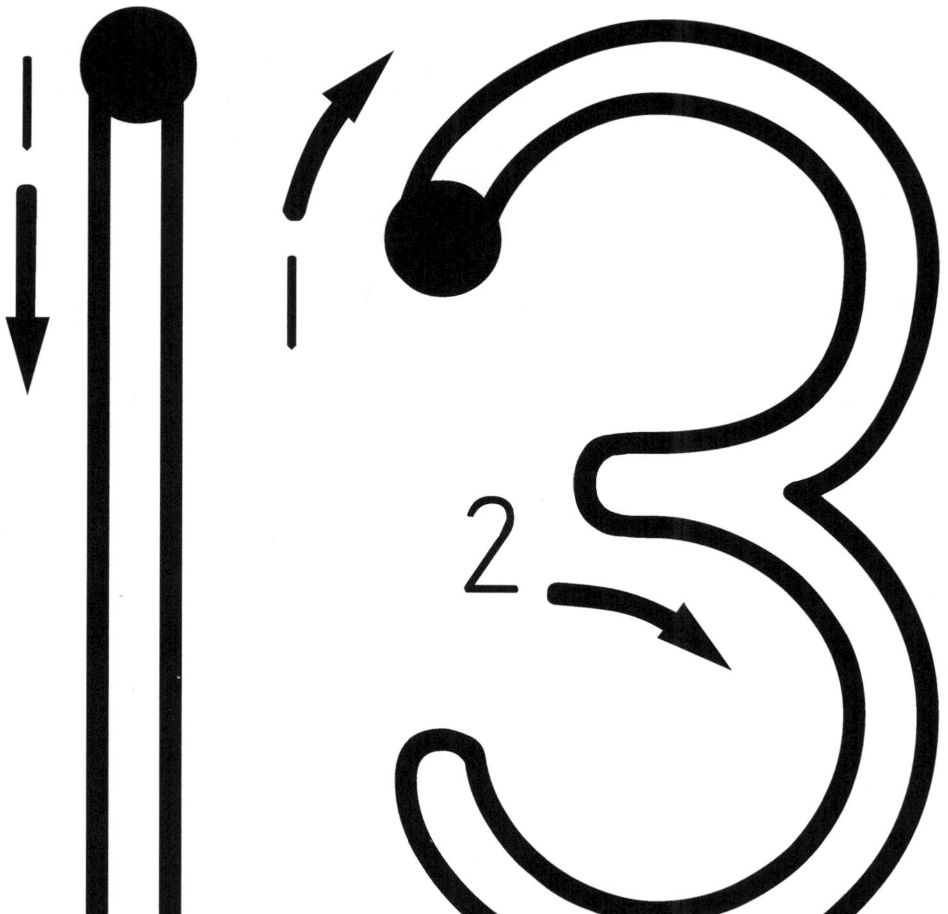

Cut along this line. Laminate or copy for extended use.

Manipulative Workmat

Use this manipulative workmat to reinforce how each number is formed.

fourteen

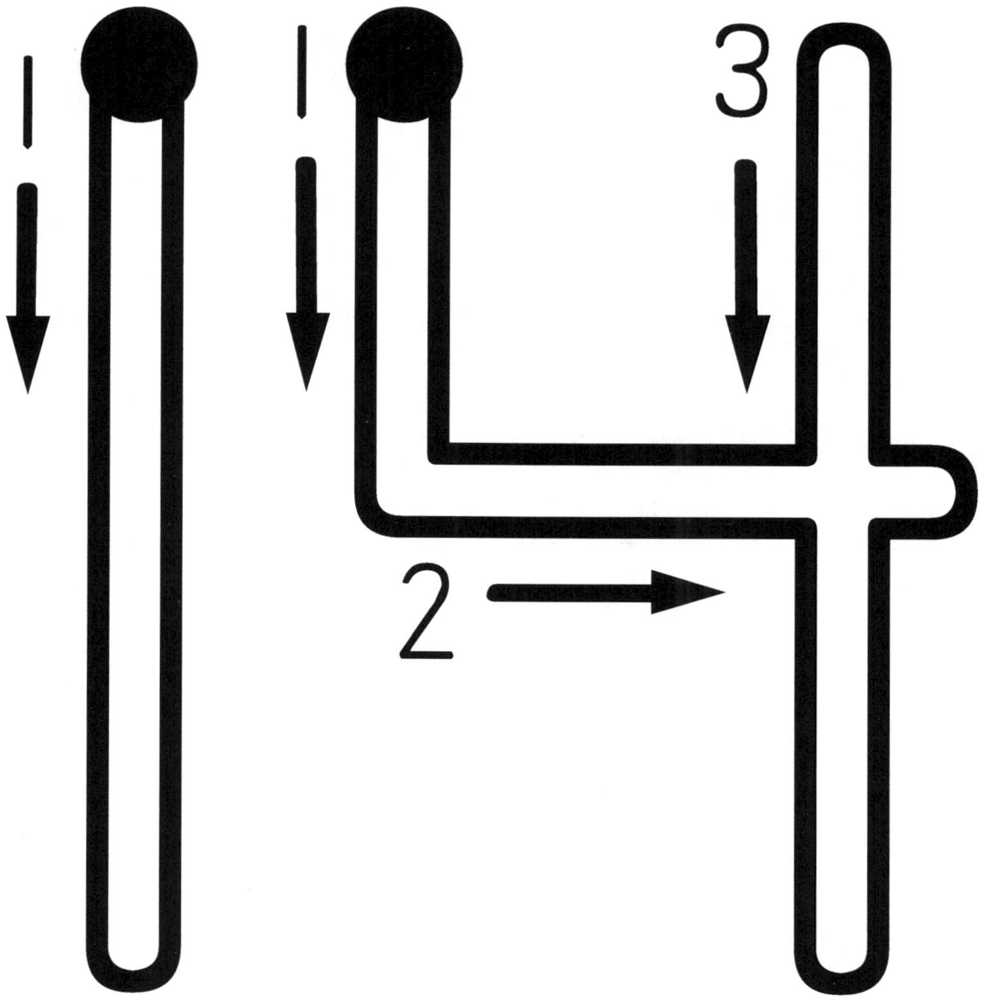

Cut along this line. Laminate or copy for extended use.

Manipulative Workmat

Use this manipulative workmat to reinforce how each number is formed.

fifteen

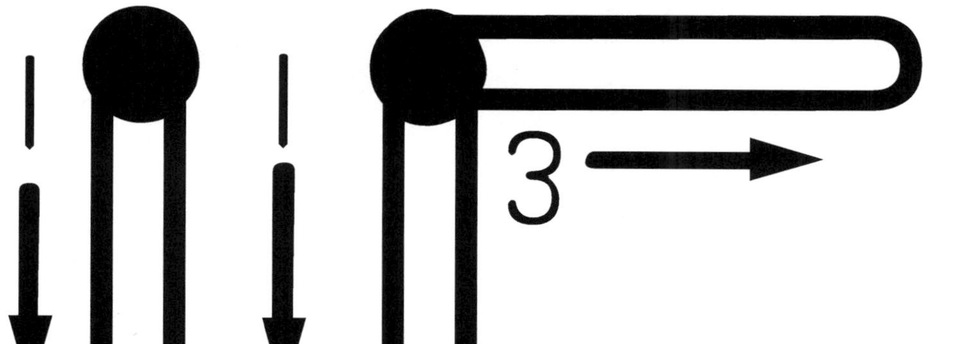

Cut along this line. Laminate or copy for extended use.

Manipulative Workmat

Use this manipulative workmat to reinforce how each number is formed.

sixteen

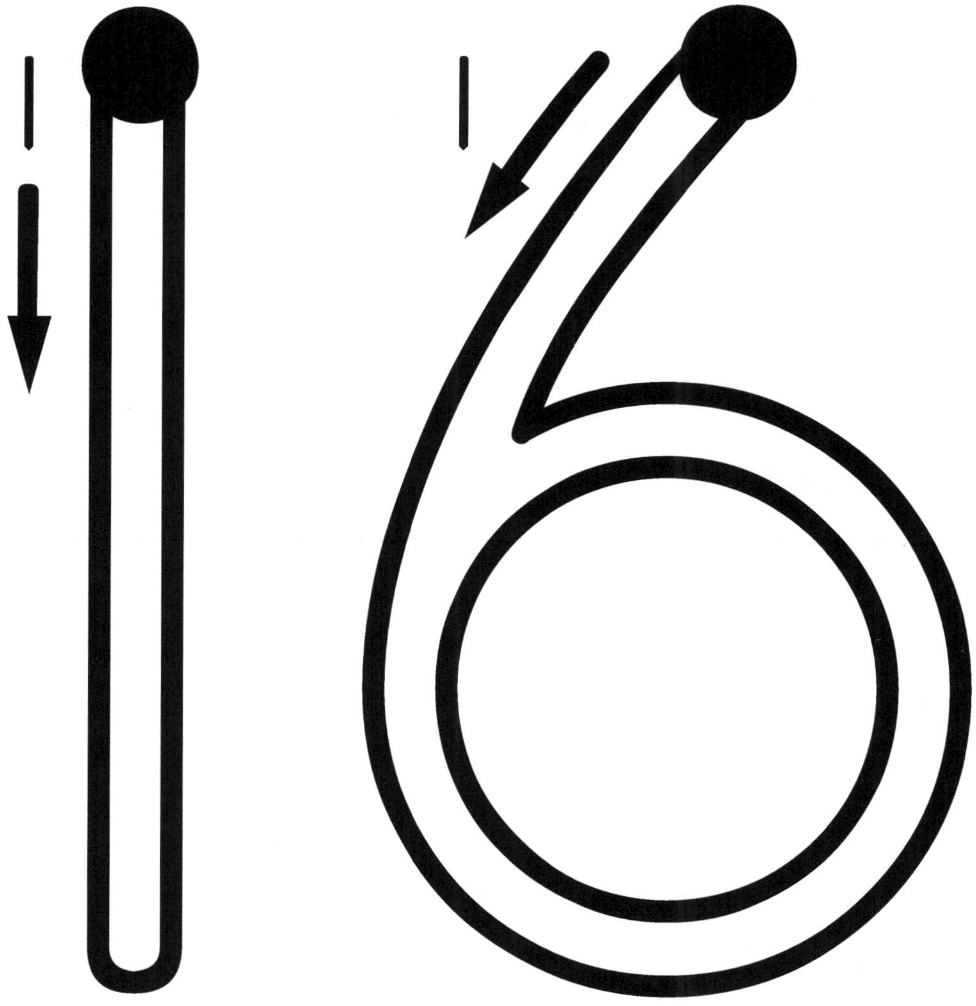

Cut along this line. Laminate or copy for extended use.

Cut along this line. Laminate or copy for extended use.

Manipulative Workmat

Use this manipulative workmat to reinforce how each number is formed.

seventeen

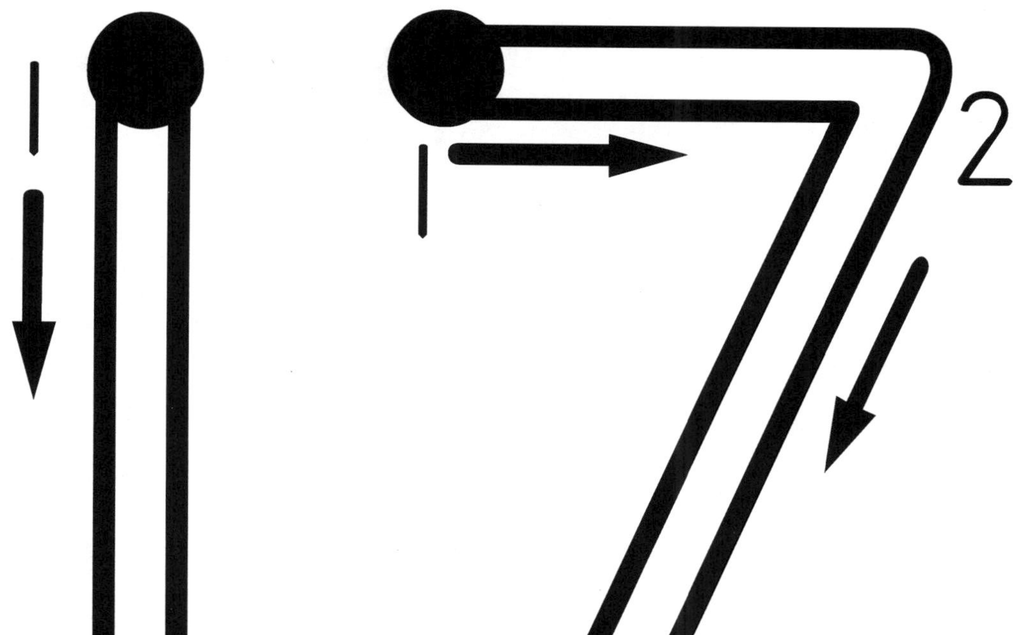

Manipulative Workmat

Use this manipulative workmat to reinforce how each number is formed.

eighteen

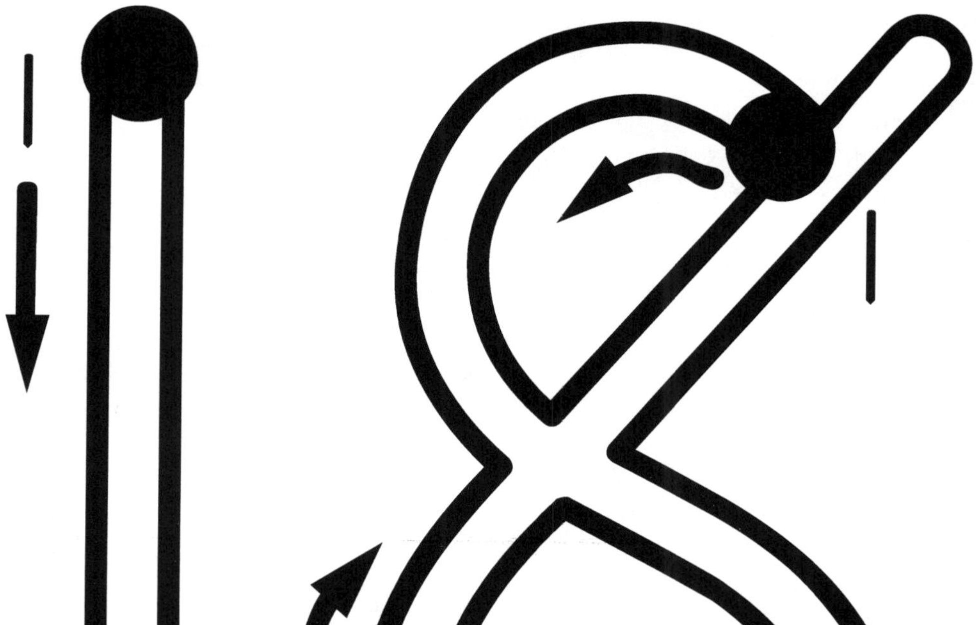

Cut along this line. Laminate or copy for extended use.

Manipulative Workmat

Use this manipulative workmat to reinforce how each number is formed.

nineteen

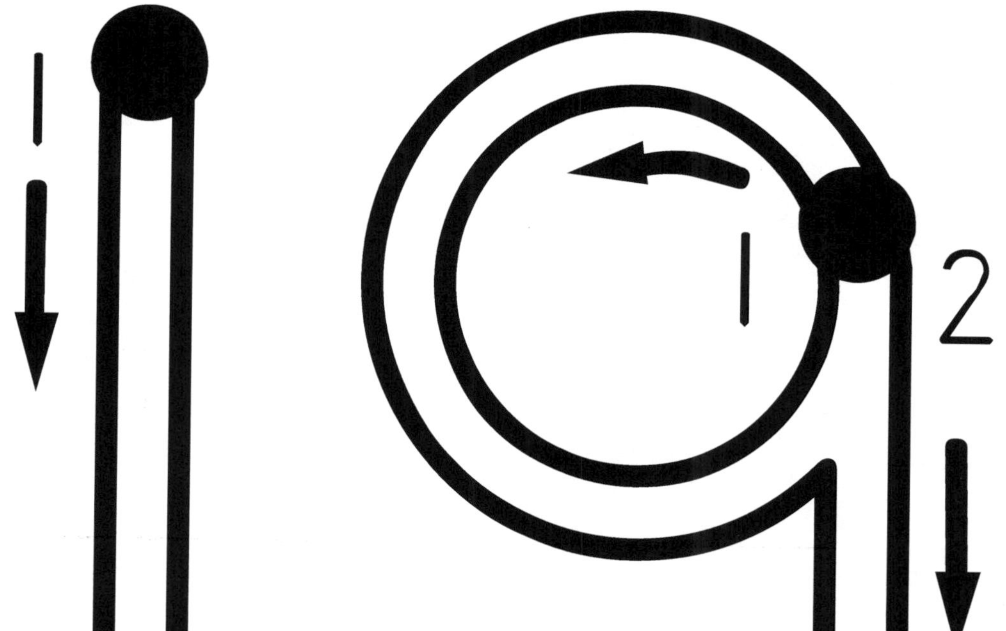

Cut along this line. Laminate or copy for extended use.

Manipulative Workmat

Use this manipulative workmat to reinforce how each number is formed.

twenty

Cut along this line. Laminate or copy for extended use.

Made in the USA
Coppell, TX
04 November 2026

11287992R00083